"A gambler's survival manual!
How To Avoid Casino Traps is
literally a step-by-step guide,
where to step, and where not to!"

— *PRN Newswire*

I walked the beach alone early this morning
hoping to find you there
but,
there was no one.
The sea is a wonderful place to drown your sorrows.
Half my life
is somewhere in the Atlantic.

—For Mary Stella Rossi

With love and appreciation, I dedicate this book to the three most important women in my life: my late mother, Mary; my loving and always supporting wife, Clare; and my granddaughter, Rachel.

HOW TO AVOID CASINO TRAPS!

JOHN ALCAMO

GOLLEHON BOOKS™
GRAND RAPIDS, MICHIGAN

Library of Congress Catalog Card Number 97-75252

ISBN 0-914839-67-5
(International Standard Book Number)

GOLLEHON BOOKS is an exclusive trademark of Gollehon
Press, Inc.

GOLLEHON BOOKS are published by: Gollehon Press, Inc.,
6157 28th St. SE, Grand Rapids, MI 49546.

GOLLEHON BOOKS are available in quantity purchases;
contact Special Sales. Gollehon does not accept unsolicited
manuscripts. Brief book proposals are reviewed.

Contents

The author wishes to express his appreciation to the dealers, pit bosses, floorpersons, casino managers, and all other casino workers who gave of their time and knowledge, my deepest gratitude goes out to you all.

To Belle, for her encouragement, support and most of all, her friendship.

To Felicia Gonzalez, for proofreading my manuscript.

A special thank you to Tom Pizzi, for introducing me to author and publisher, John Gollehon.

Editor's note...

The making of *How To Avoid Casino Traps* was a labor of love for John Alcamo. He has poured heart and soul into uncovering what really happens in a casino. He reveals the tricks and traps inside the industry which both draw us in and pick our pockets as cunningly as a thief in the night. Though his research encompasses the gaming industry throughout the entire nation, John lives and plays in Atlantic City. His nostalgia for this city he has known since childhood is best summed up in his own words:

The success of Atlantic City isn't found on some corporation's bottom line. The real prosperity is written on the faces of the people who come here. From the elderly couple on a fixed income, to the high roller with unlimited income. High roller, low roller, medium roller... they all roll into town for the same reason: the dream.

"This sure beats shuffleboard," said Sally, as she tried to draw a third ace on a quarter poker machine. Sally and her husband, Phil, celebrated their 50th wedding anniversary with a weekend trip to Atlantic City six years ago. Sally and Phil now celebrate every Monday and Thursday at Trump Plaza. Sally went on to say, "All my aches and pains disappear when I'm here. See my husband walking toward us? I can tell he won just by the way he's walking."

"How can you tell, Sally?" I asked.

"He's not using his cane."

A pair of dice, as if in slow motion, float effortlessly through the air, suspended in time, in space. Newton's theory proves to be true as the dice gently fall onto the green felt table. Ever so gently, like Jack Nicklaus hitting a nine-iron, or a ballerina dancing *The Nutcracker*; ever so softly, the dice spin around and around. You hold your breath; all eyes watching, waiting. Then, from across the concert hall, a cheer crescendos into a roar. The applause begins; the critics have spoken; the show will continue.

Before the stickman can make the call, you already know you are a winner! For a moment in time you're somebody, like Joe Montana throwing the winning touchdown pass, or Meryl Streep winning the Oscar. You have arrived. The spotlight is yours. This is what calls to us and traps us in our own greed. Step into the neon light!

The high rollers of the sea come by yachts with cute names that must have some hidden meaning to them: Ace Of My Heart, My Lucky Lady, Soft 17, Seven Come Eleven, 777. Docking in the Marina, these sea travelers come equipped with swanky clothes, jewels, a bronze tan, cats and dogs, and most importantly, *money*. They come to help balance nature by relieving the ocean of its fish population. And to help keep the economy in balance, they try to relieve the casinos of their money.

Walk through any casino and you may get the feeling that you're at the U.N. It's not unusual to hear dialect from Italy, France, Greece, or Japan—cultures that are so different from one another in language, customs, and philosophy. But they all agree on one thing: It's good when the dealer breaks.

An alarm clock in all of us rings as we drive nearer to the city. The casino's lights brighten up the skyline—red, blue, and green reflecting off the ocean. Our Boardwalk becomes a set for a Fellini movie: men in tuxedos and Nike sneakers, women in designer jeans and high heels, children with ice-cream cones and sandcastle dreams, people walking with a slice of pizza in one hand and a coin bucket in the other.

Built in 1870, the Boardwalk still holds a mystery of beauty, tradition, charm, and romance. Beneath a starbright sky, the setting is perfect for young love. Haunting melodies still echo from the days when Glenn Miller, The Dorsey Brothers, and Benny Goodman played the old Steel Pier. Music that sent a generation off to war, comes to shore with the evening tide, and only those with a sentimental ear can hear it. But tonight, everyone can hear the melodic calling of Lady Luck. After all, money won is twice as sweet as money earned.

A young boy, wearing a white summer suit, blue bow tie, and a new pair of Buster Browns, walks between his parents as they stroll the Boardwalk. Juggling a vanilla ice cream cone in one hand, and his mother's love in the other, he smiles, as the sights and sounds of a summer night go passing by.

Amusement piers, like anchored ships, harbor the shoreline. Kaleidoscope lights kidnap your imagination, and ransom your innocence. Echoing off the blue cathedral sky, there is music. An overture of hope and promise filters down the concert-hall Boardwalk. Pipe organ melodies with alluring harmonies captivate and charm a child's heart.

Children smile as they circle the world on the neon-lit carousel. Wooden horses, painted for the season and trained to be gentle, pace the merry-go-round circle. Mothers, dizzy with worry, wave as sons and daughters go spinning by.

When you're eight years old, life on the Boardwalk is an adventure. An unexplored wooden midway of enchantment and splendor. The doorway to an ocean of dreams where lighthouse eyes search for castaways lost at sea.

Eight years old, and your mind is like a sponge absorbing every drop of life. A fountain of memories that years later will quench our hearts when seasons of drought age our spirit.

Forty-five years ago, I was that eight-year-old boy.

Foreword
Caught In A Trap

A favorite topic of conversation when author John Alcamo and I connect on the telephone is not what you would expect it to be. Here we are gabbing away—two veteran gamblers—and not one mention of a hot dice table, or even a longshot that made the rent payment, or a sizzling straight flush that won the biggest pot in the poker room.

Nope. We seldom talk about boring stuff like that anymore. Today, we talk "casino marketing." The subject fascinates us! The casinos' clever, seemingly subliminal, marketing of their product monopolizes our conversations. Often, we would find ourselves playing a one-upmanship game on the telephone:

"Here's one for you. Did you know that casinos schedule their senior-citizen promotions to correspond with the dates that Social Security checks arrive in the mail?"

"I've got a better one than that! Casinos are now working with the slot manufacturers to design games that appeal to kids! Never mind that kids can't play. I guess they figure that kids will eventually become adults."

"No, they're just playing to the kids in all of us. We all like to play "kid" games. But you're right. It's almost as if they're grooming us along!"

Between the two of us, not only veteran players but veteran writers as well, we came up with at least a few dozen, but we knew there were many more hiding from us. And that was the point. They were, after all, traps. Traps are supposed to be hidden! John liked investigative writing. And, as he recalled, he liked looking for Easter eggs when he was a kid. Voila! The concept for this book was born. Born with a purpose: **to make casino players aware of what they're really up against.**

It's more than just the percentages, that's for sure. Casino players are also bucking the finest marketing ploys to rival Madison Avenue. Heck, the ad agencies on that famous stretch could take a lesson or two from a casino marketing guru! As author Alcamo often would say, "I'm telling you... the casinos know more about you than you do!"

So with the book concept in hand, John went into the trenches. To the casino bosses, the hosts, the dealers, and even the marketeers themselves, to see if he could wrestle a trick or two from what he expected to be tight-lipped, company-loyal fighters. A little wining and dining (mostly wining) and a little ego-teasing loosened the lips. That's right. Some of the casino's best broke ranks and talked openly about their trade. Pop a cork and who knows what will flow.

So will this enlightening exposé put the casino world in jeopardy? Hah! The world of casino gambling is so full of gullible, pie-in-the-sky players, so many, in fact, that we doubt if any ships will sink as a result of his book's publication. But we do know this: The signs on the casinos' doors that say "Marketing Department" should be changed to "Trap Department." The information he gathered was staggering. And even so, he doesn't claim to have found all the tricks. Otherwise, this book would have a subtitle: Volume One.

I can even tell you one he missed. One that I fondly recall from a recent trip to Las Vegas, prominently hyped from a huge sign that blasted the message into my room and into the heads of unsuspecting players within eyeshot:

CASH YOUR
PACHECK
HERE!
WIN $50,000!

I don't draw the curtains in my room when I'm out there. I want to wake up to the majesty of the mountain ranges in the distance, and the racks of hotels that fill in the valley between us. And the signs. Indeed, the signs. I want to go to bed to those same signs that come alive in the night with a message that beckons you to the window, your nose against the glass. They all say the same thing: This is Vegas. This is the *real* Vegas.

No question. There is no other city like it in the world.

For it is the mother of all come-ons; it is the side-show of all sideshows. Everything you could possibly want is there: good or bad, immoral or dull, and it is all there for you because you have something it wants. Las Vegas, you see, wants your paycheck. And it'll get it, one way or the other. The easy way or the hard way.

The casinos that cater mostly to the locals know all about cashing paychecks. They're like neighborhood banks. No free toasters, but you might get a free buffet... just so the casino can have the honor of cashing your check... *and* the honor of your presence, until seven p.m., when the ticket to win $50,000 is announced... with someone else's name on it.

The trap is so obvious. You no longer have a company check in your wallet, you have cash. Lots of cash. And you have lots of time to wait around for the big drawing. All the while there are slot machines and dice tables and poker rooms all grabbing at your money.

Casino bosses call it "walking the gauntlet." And, oh-h-h-h that is so true.

You see, the magic words are not on the big sign, they're on the back of the ticket in fine print.

MUST BE PRESENT TO WIN.

— *John Gollehon*

Introduction

I'm assuming you're a knowledgeable player but still find yourself losing more than winning. It happens to the best of players. Knowing how to play the games is only half the battle. Knowing what the casinos don't want you to know is the other half.

How To Avoid Casino Traps will give you insight that few players ever see: player's strengths and weaknesses and the casino's strengths (there are no weaknesses!) as seen through the eyes of dealers, pit bosses, casino managers, and other casino personnel. Some things players do might surprise and even amuse the more astute players. For the novice and experienced player alike, *How To Avoid Casino Traps* will be an eye-opening experience.

Gambling is no longer regarded as a social disease. It is now a social policy. State governments spend over $500 million a year advertising the lotteries. The lotteries raise over $50 billion in voluntary taxation.

Legalized gambling started in Nevada, replicated itself in Atlantic City, and then exploded across the country. Casinos seem to be everywhere: Joliet, Illinois; Michigan City and Gary, Indiana; Shreveport and Bossier City, Louisiana; Biloxi and Gulfport, Mississippi; Missouri, Connecticut, California, Michigan, Minnesota, and the list goes on. Across the Canadian border, the Casino de Montreal is among the world's ten largest casinos. Here at home, hundreds of Indian casinos compete with state-regulated casinos.

Las Vegas, the patriarch of the casino industry, ever so carefully watches its offspring flourish. Not to be outdone, construction equipment can be seen almost everywhere in this fastest-growing city in the nation. Old casinos are being demolished to make way for bigger and flashier new ones. Walk down the Strip and you can see exploding volcanoes, dueling pirates, dueling mummies, dueling knights, and even dueling cabdrivers in front of New York, New York. (That's New York, New York, THE CASINO.) A retired dealer and lifelong resident of Las Vegas said to me, "The whole damn town looks like one big theme park."

"Gambling in America is a supermarket," said Steve Wynn, former Chairman of the Board for Mirage Resorts, Inc. "It's a robust, whop 'em, sock 'em, screaming, table-pounding, yahoo, c'mon dice, jump up and down when you hit a jackpot. We're out to capture the fancy of Middle America, out to have fun, and raise a little hell."

More than 75 percent of Americans gamble. Who are these thrill seekers and where do they come from? They're young and old, the rich and famous, the couple next door, the haves and have-nots. Twenty-five years ago only two states had legalized casino gambling. Today, gambling is available is some form in every state except two: Hawaii and Utah.

U.S. News & World Report published the following statement from a government study: "Gambling, whether it is legal or illegal, appears to provide an escape from frustrated ambitions by offering the hope of a better life to people who otherwise have little expectation of improving their socioeconomic status. From this point of view, provision of a legal outlet can be construed as fulfilling a social need."

"Honey, take the kids to the snack bar and buy them ice cream. I'm going over to that blackjack table to fulfill my social need."

Why do you gamble? Have you ever asked yourself that question? Is it the adrenalin rush? The excitement of the games? Are you reaching for the pie-in-the-sky jackpot that can change your life forever? Is it the challenge of beating the casino at its own game?

Day or night, the excitement in a casino knows no timetable, no season. Who among us can deny that ecstatic feeling you get when dealt a blackjack? Or the instant recognition as strangers gather around your bell-ringing slot machine. Players rooting you on at the craps table after you've made seven passes in a row.

Where else can you see thousands of dollars being won or lost by the turning of a card or the toss of the dice? The casino is exciting and unpredictable. Win or lose, gambling shows us a side of ourselves we never knew existed. It's an emotional roller-coaster ride.

There is one thing you can bet on: Gambling is here to stay. Card rooms, horse racing, dog tracks, lottery terminals, bingo halls, sports-betting parlors, and casinos are quenching America's thirst for the quick buck. (Notice I didn't say, "*easy* buck"!)

Casinos separate players into three categories: the high roller, the medium roller, and the low roller. But for the players themselves there are only two categories: winners and losers! In what category do *you* belong?

Cash dominates a casino. It's the casino's life blood. And every day of the year players eager for the quick score become donors. On a day-to-day basis, there is no other business that handles the abundance of coins and paper money that circulates through a casino. Banks don't even come close. Hydraulic lifts are used to move the stacks of cash and coins from the casino floor to the casino's count room. Tons of it.

In the old days, people actually counted the money by hand. Today, modern technology has made this task easier. The money is weighed. A million dollars in $100 bills weighs 20 and one-half pounds; a million in $20s, 102 pounds; a million dollars in quarters weighs 21 tons.

Casinos have the statistics and their ever-increasing bottom-line to back up the fact that over 95% of all players anticipate a loss the minute they walk in the door! Casinos bank on it, literally, every day.

Maybe some of these comments will help you understand why:

FROM AN ATLANTIC CITY PIT BOSS: "Over the long term, casinos can mold a player into developing losing habits and a losing attitude."

FROM A RIVERBOAT DICE SUPERVISOR: "I never saw such a business where people were so anxious to give you their money. Give them a free drink and a dream, and they'll give you their wallets."

FROM A LAKE TAHOE CASINO HOST: "We win because players have no winning goal in mind. When they're ahead, they want more. And eventually they give it all back."

FROM A LAS VEGAS CASINO MANAGER: "Very few players take the time to keep an accurate record of their winnings and losses. I know for certain that if they did they would be on the losing end. But every time they buy in or sit down at a slot machine, they wipe the slate clean. They like to start fresh. They like to pretend they're even."

FROM A PROFESSIONAL GAMBLER: "A very small majority of players show an uncompromising discipline. It's not always the game that defeats the player, it's greed and ego. The players defeat themselves."

Do you see yourself in some of these quotes?

A casino manager once told me, "The greatest quote I ever heard was from legendary circus owner P. T. Barnum. Barnum said, 'There's a sucker born every minute.' If Barnum were a casino owner, he would have said, 'There's a sucker born every *second!*'"

So hurry, hurry, hurry! Step right up, ladies and gentlemen! Let's go behind the tables and find out how to be a winner in the biggest circus of all: The Casino!

CHAPTER 1

What The Casinos Won't Tell You

Most how-to books written about gambling focus on a player's offense. Knowing how to play and how to structure your bets are your first steps in the right direction. But just pointing you in the right direction isn't enough. **To be a winner, you must also be a strong defensive player.** And that's what this book is mostly about.

"The Best Offense Is A Good Defense"

A winning Super Bowl coach once said, "The best offense is a good defense." In a roundabout way, the overall opinion from the casino insiders I've talked to is similar to the football coach's statement. One casino

CEO said, "I've seen some of the best offensive players in the world go down the tubes. And their downfall had nothing to do with bad luck or insignificant playing techniques. Their lack of defensive playing tactics gave us the opportunity to beat them."

The players will always be the underdogs and the casinos will always be the odds-on favorites. But casinos are not unbeatable dynasties, at least not in the short term. If you know how to avoid the traps they set for you, you *can* win! It's not an impossibility unless you allow them to intimidate you... to lure you... to take your control away.

Play smart. But above all, play defensively.

Knowledge Is Power

If you want to be a strong player, it's up to you to educate yourself. "It's amazing how many people take a lazy approach to gambling," said a dealer. "They simply don't do their homework. Most players are totally ignorant of the games and percentages against them. They buy into a dream, not the game. The dream of getting something for nothing. A fast way to make a buck. Well, the only people making a fast buck in a casino today are the stockholders."

Indeed. When it comes to buying a car or home appliance, you search for the best price. You spend time, researching the product. Why not take the same approach to casino gambling?

The growing popularity of casino gambling has shown no signs of slowing down. Today, land-based and riverboat casinos continue to proliferate. Corporate ownership and theme resorts have made gambling an acceptable American pastime.

Casino gambling outdraws sporting events, concerts, and Broadway shows. Atlantic City, as a whole, draws more visitors than DisneyWorld. On a busy weekend in Vegas, nearly 200,000 people enter the neon gates, nearly busting the town at its seams. It's hard to believe, but it's true. Oh, there's a market out there, a huge market of players who need to be educated. This chapter will address the hard line of casino gambling. I'll show you the true percentages and expose the issues that casinos shy away from.

Everyone I interviewed for this chapter has at least 20 years of casino employment under his or her belt—dealers, supervisors, pit bosses, casino hosts, credit managers, and casino managers. Collectively, they have over 500 years of casino experience. Sometimes, depending on the question, their opinions on gambling differed and our round-table discussions turned into heated debates.

There was one thing however that the entire panel did agree on. No one knew or had heard of a single player who has won money at any casino game over an extended period of time!

"Your readers won't like hearing this," said a casino host, "but the slots and table games are virtually unbeatable over the long term. Why? Because when the odds are against you on every bet in a game, there is no system in the world that can consistently beat the game."

"Correct," said a casino VP. "If you ever read about a casino in financial trouble, don't think for one minute that the players had anything to do with it. Usually it's mismanagement or start-up costs that cause the problems."

But it wasn't always that way.

Breaking The Bank

In 1946, at a small private gambling club in Miami Beach, a woman held the dice for two hours, costing the club $500,000. The club owner's bankroll was completely depleted, forcing him to close the table *and* the club. But could this happen in one of today's corporate-run casinos?

FROM A LAS VEGAS PIT BOSS: "From time to time you might read a story about someone's winning millions of dollars from a casino. The casino's publicity department is eager to give this information to the newspapers. But the casinos only give the newspapers half of the story. They never release the follow-up story about the same player who eventually loses all of his or her winnings, plus, money out of his or her pockets. I never met a big winner who walked off into the sunset and never returned."

FROM A VICE PRESIDENT OF CASINO OPERA-TIONS IN INDIANA: "Casinos, if run properly, never allow themselves to be vulnerable to the occasional winning streak that from time to time shifts to the player's side of the table. Even in the good old days when a casino might have been owned and operated by one individual, the risk of a casino going belly-up was small. For today's corporate-run casinos, the risk of some wealthy player or a group of wealthy players breaking the house is impossible. Why? Because as long as a casino keeps an adequate amount of money on hand and religiously sticks to rules of the game, the casino has nothing to worry about.

"No player can avoid the 'per.' The percentage against the player is uncompromising. The risk of going broke is always on the player's side of the table. In other words, the only bank in jeopardy of being broken is yours."

The term *breaking the bank* is misleading. It doesn't mean that a player has won all the money in a casino. Sometimes you might see the action at a hot table stop momentarily for a chip refill because the starting bank at that table has been exhausted. Remember, though, that the bank at each table is only a small fraction of the casino's total bank. But it wasn't always that way.

There's a song called "The Man Who Broke The Bank At Monte Carlo." It was written about a man named Charles Well, who in 1891 won so much money that he became a celebrity in Europe. Because of his success, he was rubbing elbows with aristocrats on the French

Riviera and dining with kings and queens. One year and countless hours of roulette play later, he was broke. When patrons at the fashionable resort inquired about Charles's well-being, they were told that he was living in France. That was half of the truth. The other half was that Charles was homeless and living on the streets.

FROM A CONNECTICUT SHIFT BOSS: "Casinos tolerate winners because they know that, in the long term, no player is a threat to the casino's enormous bankroll. The news of a big win spreads quickly through a casino and lures more players to the tables, hoping for the big score. In the meantime, the lucky player is given the red-carpet treatment: food, wine, room, clothes, jewelry... basically, whatever it takes to keep the player from going home. Keeping a winner happy and a loser hopeful, that's the silent edge we never talk about."

A pit boss told me the story about a player who parlayed $500 into $105,000. "It started with a hot hand at the craps table. The player started with $500 and left the table with $42,000. Then he table-hopped: blackjack, baccarat, roulette... it didn't matter because whatever he touched turned to gold. In all my years in this business I've never seen anything like it. We gave him every comp imaginable just to keep him in the hotel. Three days later he went home with $50. We accept the fact that sometimes players will win large sums of money. But we try our best to keep them from walking out the door with our money."

Does everybody love a winner? It's human nature for most of us to root for the underdog. In other words, the player. I've never seen a group of players rooting for the casino. And I doubt that I ever will. Like waitresses and bartenders, a dealer depends on tokes (tips) to make a living. So, naturally, a dealer will embrace a winning player as long as that player is toking the dealer. But some shift bosses couldn't care less about a dealer's livelihood.

"For me," said one shift boss, who reminded me of actor George C. Scott in the movie *Patton*, "the casino floor is a battleground. It's us against you; and whoever has the most money at the end of the battle is the victor. From time to time we may have a slight setback, but that's only temporary. The player might be skilled and even a little lucky. But the longer the battle goes on, his skill and luck are no longer a threat because we have the most reliable weapon: house advantage. Each game has a built-in house advantage that won't budge, no matter how outnumbered we are."

Playing The Odds

Every casino has instructional booklets explaining the rules and how to play a particular game. But these booklets never fully explain to the player the correct odds on every bet. For example, let's take what I consider to be the most obvious misconception players have about odds. In the casino's booklet on roulette they tell you that the payoff for hitting a number straight up is 35 to 1. On a double-zero roulette wheel there are 38 numbers. The correct payoff should be 37 to 1. This information is not found in that little casino booklet. It also doesn't tell you that this "shortage" (two out of 38 or 1/19) is worth 5.26 percent to the house.

FROM A MISSISSIPPI ROULETTE DEALER: "To make the player get more involved in the game, some casinos have a gigantic scoreboard hooked up to the roulette table that displays the past winning numbers. Some players like to write down the numbers themselves and try to analyze the wheel. A dealer or floorperson will gladly give the player a scorecard so the player can track the so-called hot or due numbers. There is no such thing as a due number. I get a kick out of players saying that a number or color is due as if the wheel had ears. If a number doesn't hit after 50 spins, this does not reduce the odds of that same number hitting within the next 50 spins, or even 100 spins. The odds are always the same."

"So, does a scorecard help the player or the house?" I asked. "Subconsciously," said the dealer, "the casino is giving you something else to think about instead of the game's high percentage against you. Instead of handing out scorecards, the casino should hand you a note saying: THE ROULETTE WHEEL WILL ALWAYS PROVIDE A RANDOM DISTRIBUTION OF WINNING NUMBERS. PREVIOUS WINNING NUMBERS HAVE NO EFFECT ON FUTURE OUTCOMES. THE WHEEL HAS NO MEMORY."

One interesting thing I've noticed is that players tracking the wheel tend to play longer. Notice I didn't say that they were winning. Tracking the wheel gives them a false sense of hope that they can outsmart the wheel. And with a 5.26 percent house advantage, that's exactly what the casino wants. The longer you play, the more likely you'll lose. Why? It's worth repeating: Because casinos do not pay correct odds on any roulette wager! They pay a little less. You really didn't expect them to pay a little *more*, did you?

FROM A LAS VEGAS ROULETTE DEALER: "A roulette player will never win in the long term. It's mathematically impossible. The world's most brilliant mathematicians have all come to the same conclusion concerning roulette and other games of chance. In the long term, the game is unbeatable and there isn't a casino instructional booklet in the world that will tell you that."

FROM A KENO RUNNER: "Technically speaking, keno is a lottery. It's a low roller's dream game that quickly becomes a $2 bettor's nightmare. The fatal attraction of a game like keno is the possibility of winning a large sum of money that will solve all your financial problems. If a player plays a 10-spot for $2 and hits all ten numbers, the player wins $100,000. But the odds of hitting ten out of ten are nearly 9 million to 1! I've been a keno runner for 24 years and I haven't paid off a 10-spot yet. Now that I think about it, I haven't paid off any tickets bigger than an eight-out-of-eight 8-spot, and I think I only did that twice!

"Some players mistakenly compare keno to bingo. But there is one very important difference between the two games. A bingo game ends only when someone hits the grand prize for that game. This is not the case in keno. The only guaranteed winner after all the numbers are drawn in keno is the casino."

FROM A KENO SUPERVISOR: "Table games like craps, blackjack, roulette, and baccarat produce a larger handle for the casino. But keno gives the casino a higher hold percentage. The house advantage in keno is never lower than 25 percent and can be as high as 40 percent depending on the type of wager a player makes. Casinos have a love-hate relationship with keno. The game is slow, the bets are small, and the cost of running the game is high. On the other hand, keno is money in the bank for the casino."

Have you ever read the cover of a keno brochure? It might read something like this: DISCOVER HOW EASY PLAYING AND WINNING AT KENO CAN BE! Obviously the brochure is only telling you half the truth. It doesn't tell you the casino keeps your initial bet, which means it will not pay you the true odds. If you play a 1-spot ticket for $5 and hit it, the casino payoff is $15, five dollars of which was yours in the first place. Since the true odds are 3 to 1, the payoff should be $20. What the casino isn't telling you in the keno brochure is that the casino has changed the payoff to 2 to 1.

The Sting

FROM A RETIRED CASINO MANAGER: "I firmly believe that the minute players walk into the casino they lose all sense of reality and logic. We have created a fantasy world where fame and fortune, like lightning, can strike at any moment. Pictures of smiling jackpot winners cover the walls leading into the casino and subconsciously tell the player: This could be you! You know what they say, 'A picture is worth a thousand words.' For a casino, those pictures are worth millions of dollars in slot revenue."

FROM A GULFPORT CRAPS DEALER: "I suspect that most craps players are masochists. Because if they knew the correct odds of the game, no one would make a place-bet, a field-bet, or a prop-bet, especially hardways or elevens. But thousands and thousands of players do. Some prop-bets give the house a 16 percent advantage over the player. It's ridiculous, but they like the big payoffs on these tougher bets. That's why the house advantage is so high on these bets. Because the casino knows that players love to make them!"

FROM A LAS VEGAS CRAPS DEALER: "Craps isn't a complex game. I think people shy away from a craps table because the layout looks so confusing. But the game is really simple. Bet the pass-line and take the full odds behind your pass-line bet. Make come-bets and take the full odds. That's it. That's all you need to know. Because if you make any other bet on that table, you're throwing money away."

FROM A RENO CRAPS DEALER: "I've been dealing craps eight hours a day, five days a week, for 22 years. Sometimes the dice get a little wacky and the house gets hurt. I've seen the occasional hot roll where players parlayed $100 hardways and pressed numbers until they hit the table max. But in the long run, the dice always correct themselves. If they didn't, I'd be out of a job."

FROM AN ATLANTIC CITY PIT BOSS: "The atmosphere in the casino can be intoxicating. A casino is like a treasure chest filled with money and everyone is hoping to find the key. Players seem to put a different label on money. Fifty dollars, a hundred dollars, or a thousand dollars diminishes in value, especially at a craps table where a multitude of bets are offered and the pace of the game is fast. When I see a player, who normally never makes a prop-bet, start throwing money into that fairy-tale land in the center of the table, I know that the player has lost touch with reality."

If you must make prop-bets, read the table layout carefully. Casinos disguise the correct payoffs by using the word *for* instead of *to*. If the table layout on a hard 4 or 10 reads 8 for 1, don't be misled. The word *for* means you don't keep your bet. The word *to* means you do keep your bet. 8 for 1 is the same as 7 to 1.

Still, there are times when a gambler can still believe in Santa Claus. Read on.

FROM A CALIFORNIA POKER DEALER: "There was a great old-time poker player who hit a long losing streak. For the first time in his life he was broke. He was driving a cab in Vegas, hoping to save enough money to get a gambling bankroll together. In between fares one night he stopped at a casino, bought a keno ticket, and walked over to the coffee shop for the 99-cent breakfast special. The waitress took his order but never saw him again. While his eggs were frying, he glanced at the keno board and saw his six numbers. In his shirt pocket was a five-dollar 6-spot ticket. He picked up $7,500 and headed straight for the poker room. He won about $12,000 that night on my table. I haven't seen him in years, but I've heard through the grapevine that the guy now owns a fleet of taxicabs!"

Why Do So Many Players Lose?

FROM A MISSOURI BLACKJACK DEALER: "We win because players have no rigid game plan. Let's not even talk about the dumb players who have no idea how to play the games. I'm talking about the so-called smart players. Whether they play blackjack, craps, roulette, baccarat, whatever the game, they have a way of turning whatever knowledge they have about the game against them.

"If a player plays long enough, whether he's winning or losing, something happens to that player's common sense. Reality goes out the window. There's something about being in a casino that weakens the strongest of players, and that's when a player becomes vulnerable. Winners get drunk on greed. Losers make foolish bets. They bet on hunches and feelings. The longer players stay at a table or a machine, the easier it is for us to break them down. Even if it's one dollar at a time."

FROM AN INDIAN CASINO MANAGER IN MICHIGAN: "There are very few hit-and-run players. Over the years, casinos have done a wonderful job of conditioning people to believe that gambling is simply a recreational experience. They called it *gambling*, then *gaming*; now they call it *entertainment*. It simply amazes me how gullible some people are. It's gotten to the point that losing in a casino is acceptable. And that's exactly the attitude casino owners want the public to have."

FROM AN ATLANTIC CITY EXECUTIVE OF SLOT OPERATIONS: "Today, it would seem that it's not necessarily whether you win or lose, but how long you can play. If you have a bankroll of $100 and you can play with that for an hour and a half, that's considered entertainment. But the hundred's gone. A player... ANY player, should never write off a gambling loss as entertainment. That's too easy."

Behind The Glitz And Glamour

FROM A LAS VEGAS PIT BOSS: "Over the years, the ambience of a casino has changed. A casino tries to do everything in its power to distract the player from the reality of casino gambling. In some casinos, it starts the minute a customer walks in. Lobby entertainers, clowns handing out balloons, it feels more like an amusement park than a casino. The casino is setting the mood. It's altering the player's demeanor. It's creating a party atmosphere to help soften the blow when players lose money. The last thing a casino wants players to do is to dwell on how much money they've lost while they're still on the casino's property. Keeping the players entertained is our psychological pain killer."

FROM A CONNECTICUT CASINO EXECUTIVE: "People get lost in the glitz and glamour. They come here to escape life's daily routine. And we give them the escape route that they're looking for. Believe me when I say that over 95 percent of the people who go to casinos are not skilled players. They anticipate a loss before they make their first bet. And, not surprisingly, they go home losers."

The Truth About Comps

Getting something for nothing. That's the attitude most players have about "comps." But the casino industry is not in the habit of giving something away for nothing.

Casinos are not giving away the store to get new players or to keep their regular players happy. The general public may still have that perception, and that's exactly what casinos count on. How does a casino decide whether or not you warrant a comp? The whole "comp criteria" is probably the most misunderstood element of casino gambling.

Comps can have such a negative effect on players, particularly table players, that I want to expose the shortcomings in this chapter and then cover other interesting sidelines of casino complimentaries in the next chapter, too.

The comp phenomenon started in Las Vegas in the mid '50s. After the federal government started closing down illegal gambling joints, Las Vegas answered by opening up legal ones. When the Riviera, the Dunes, the Desert Inn, and the New Frontier opened, Las Vegas became this country's first legitimate casino resort destination. Comps were used to attract players.

The shift boss had the power of the pen. "It was simply an unwritten law," said a retired shift boss, "If a player's action warranted it, that player would get a comped room, meals, show tickets, and airfare. If I had an action player, I'd do anything to keep him at our tables."

Nevada had no competition until 1978 when Resorts Hotel Casino opened in New Jersey. That's when the whole concept of comps changed forever.

FROM A RETIRED VEGAS SHIFT BOSS: "Keep in mind that I come from a different era. In the '50s, Wall Street corporations weren't involved. Casinos were smaller. Our overhead was low. Today, you have mega-resorts with enormous overhead. With casino gambling almost everywhere, people are becoming more and more demanding. They expect to be comped the minute they walk in. Comps are like a double-edged sword. If a casino gives away the store in an effort to lure players, they could face some serious financial problems down the road. On the other hand, a casino doesn't want to offend a player and risk losing a customer. For a casino to succeed, comps are essential. But the concept behind a comp is simple. I learned a long time ago that where players eat, sleep, and drink, that's where they'll gamble. Keeping players at the tables and making them feel like they're getting something for nothing, that's what this business is all about. There isn't a college textbook in the world that will teach you that."

FROM AN ILLINOIS HOST: "Twenty years ago I was working in Lake Tahoe, and I had a player who was a pain in the ass. He was never happy. I'd comp him a room, and he'd ask for a suite. If I gave him two show tickets, he'd ask for six. He was an average player, and his play didn't justify the comps he'd ask for. This went on for years. Then one night it happened. That proverbial score that players dream about. Between craps, blackjack, and a slot machine jackpot, his $500 bankroll mushroomed into $66,000. Money does do strange things to people. For years, this player's highest bet was $10. But that night, he became a $100 pass-line bettor.

"All night long it was comp me this, comp me that. If I gave him a suite, he complained that it was too small. I comped him four tickets to see Sinatra, and he wanted ten. Naturally, the casino wanted him to stay, so I'm comping him like there's no tomorrow. Two days later we got the $66,000 back, and he had to wire home for airfare money.

"The moral of my story is easy: Don't play for comps. Play for money. Don't think that we're giving you comps because we have a big heart. This business is all about money. It's *your* money against *our* money. And if you win, we'll smile and be gracious. A comp is like a magnet. It keeps players where we want them. At the tables!"

The last sentence in the above paragraph is very important because what he's really saying is that by keeping a player at the tables, that player stays vulnerable. The player's money is at risk. The casino edge is concrete. A player's luck is iffy.

All casino games have a specific house advantage that over the years has been proven flawless.

Getting Rated
(Or Should That Be "Raided"?)

When a casino "rates" a player, it uses a mathematical formula to determine the player's hypothetical loss.

Keep in mind that the purpose of this formula is not for the casino to keep a record of your winnings or losses; the casino wants to know the *value* of your play.

Basically, the casino wants to know your average bet, hours played, speed of the game, and house advantage. Toss them all together and they equal your hypothetical loss, which will determine the amount of your comp. Win or lose, if your play warrants it, you will be comped.

Some casinos, however, do consider the *way* players play by looking at the kind of bets they make, their temperament and style (reckless, aggressive, or conservative, for example), and even the player's skill, particularly as it might apply to blackjack. For example, a card-counter might reduce the house advantage—but probably not by much, if any—so the casino will make minor adjustments in that player's theoretical loss.

Remember that when you lose, you are not losing "theoretical" money. You're losing "real" money. If you go to a casino on a regular basis, don't even ask to be rated. When you sit at a table, ignore the pit boss or floorperson who might ask to rate you. Asking for a rating is the first step in asking for trouble.

For those players who won't heed my advice, at least don't let comps interfere with your playing habits. Remember, you're playing to win money, not a free dinner or free room. If comps were a losing proposition, casinos would have stopped giving them out a long time ago. Believe me when I say that comps are one of the biggest hooks casinos use to get at your money.

A Word From Three Wise Men

Allow me to close this chapter with something else that casinos won't tell you. The following stories all relate to professional players who have mastered those few games that *can* be beaten over time. Let's let the players themselves tell their stories:

The man sitting across from me in the casino coffee shop is a true professional gambler. He's not a craps, blackjack, or baccarat player. And certainly not a slot player. His game is poker. Seven-card stud. Like most players who make their living gambling, he wishes to remain anonymous. So let's just call him "Bluff."

It's almost 5 a.m. and Bluff just finished playing. (Bluff calls it "working.") He'd been playing (working) for 16 hours that day. "I make a modest living. I'll never be a great player or big-money player like Johnny Moss, Amarillo Slim, or this young kid from New York, Stu Ungar. Even though he's in his 40s, I still call him a kid. Hell, I'm 76. Besides knowing the game, to be successful you must know and respect your own limitations. In other words, you can't play over your head. You'll never catch me at the same table with Doyle Brunson, Bobby Baldwin, or Puggy Pearson. They're way out of my league."

When Bluff was 13 years old, he was a go-for in an illegal poker parlor in Boston. "That's where I learned the game," said Bluff. "The joint also had a craps game in the back room. I learned something there, too. Craps can't be beaten on a steady basis."

Bluff told me that his yearly income from playing poker runs between $25,000 to $30,000 per year. "It's not big money. But it sure beats punching a clock from 9 to 5."

Bluff spent most of his gambling life playing poker in Nevada and card rooms in California. He had some very strong opinions on the subject of casino games. "There are no weak casino games. Every game dominates the player. In poker, a player can dominate the game and the weaker players. To make money at this game, a player needs skill, talent, instincts, and experience. You could have all the skill and talent in the world and there ain't a casino in the world that won't let you play. That should tell you something."

Bluff was visiting relatives in the Boston area when the Foxwoods Casino opened in Connecticut. "I heard they had a poker room, so I went over for a look-see. I loved what I saw. Tables full of recreational poker players. I did recognize some players from Nevada and California, and they were having a field day. I was looking at a gold mine. The only drawback was the long wait for a seat at a table."

Poker, in a casino setting, is the only game where player is pitted against player. The casino has no edge. They supply the table, cards, dealer, refreshments and ensure the game's integrity. The casino gets a "rake" on lower-limit games that may not exceed 10 percent of the pot.

The last time Bluff was in Atlantic City was 1952. But when the Showboat Casino Hotel opened Atlantic

City's first poker room in 1993, Bluff left Connecticut. In Atlantic City, Bluff and his other poker-playing friends do very well.

"The weekend poker players don't know the first thing about reading their opponents. When they're out of the hand, they're looking at the ball game on television. I always study the other players. Watching them while they play tells me a lot about them. When I'm in a poker game, the outside world is a million miles away."

According to Bluff, very few poker players can make a living at it. "Learning the game isn't that difficult. But getting a feeling for the game is. You could read book after book about poker, but no one can teach you intuition, patience, or self-control. I have my losing streaks like everyone else who does this for a living. But I also have the confidence that I'll come back and end the year on the winning side."

Sports Betting

"I bet professional football and NOTHING else," said Lee. "I have always believed that if you want to be a professional gambler you have to zero in on one game. And for me, it's football."

Lee wasn't always a full-time gambler. He has a master's degree in history and taught at some of the nation's leading universities. "I always loved football, but I was never big enough to play," said Lee. "When I was a teenager, I had a notebook full of statistics. The players, teams, coaches, injury list, trades, and so on. Today I do the same thing, but now I use a computer."

Casino sports books in Nevada have seen a steady rise in business. Football attracts the most action. Some sports books in Vegas are handling over $40 million a year in business, and depending on the game, the casino "juice "(or hold) is between 2 and 5 percent. When betting on football or basketball, you wager $11 for every $10 you want to win. The casino keeps the extra dollar on losing tickets, which they call the juice.

"When I was in college, I used to make small bets with the guys. I never took the betting part seriously until a friend of mine talked me into going to Las Vegas for a long weekend. The minute I stepped into the betting parlor, I knew this would become my new home."

After Lee returned home from his long weekend, he quit his teaching job, sold his house, and moved to Vegas. "I sold everything: my house, my car, and stocks and bonds that have been in the family for years. I wanted to have a competitive bankroll, which I knew was just as important as my skill for handicapping football."

That was 15 years ago, and Lee has never looked back. "I'm doing very well. I'm a very cautious gambler. I never make parlay bets. I stay away from teaser bets and gimmick bets like the over-and-under. Some Sundays I don't bet at all. If I don't like the spread, I don't bet. When you're gambling to put food on the table and pay the bills, you've got to have self-control." Lee works hard at what he does. "My year starts the

day the players report to training camp. I read all the
major sports magazines and newspapers. I file every bit
of information that I think is important into my computer. I have only two rules that I never break: (1) I
never bet a game for the sole purpose of getting even,
and (2) I never tell my friends what teams I'm betting."

The Stretch Run

"When I was a kid, I worked as a stable-hand every
summer. But I always wanted to be a jockey," said
Louie. "But, as you can see, I've got a weight problem."

For his size, Louie's a very soft-spoken guy. "I have
to be honest with you, betting the horses ain't what it
use to be. I can tell you why in one word: *taxes*. Even
in Nevada, for example, the racebooks are virtually all
parimutuel, so they take out 18 to 22 percent just like
the tracks do. On a straight bet, that's bad enough. And
I only make straight bets. But it gets worse for the poor
slob who likes to bet the exotics like pick-6."

Louie, like most gamblers I know, isn't a bragger.
Looking at him, you'd never know if he's winning or
losing. He's secure and confident about what he does.

"I can't explain to you how I do what I do in two
days. It has taken me years to get to this point. Gambling for a living is different from other occupations. If
you have a regular job and you're just an average
worker, you still get paid. But in this profession, the
mediocre go broke fast."

I did spend one day at the track with Louie. It was a ten-race card, but Louie was there to bet only two races. "I only like two horses today," said Louie as he buried his head in the racing form. He wasn't writing down much. "I do my homework all night. I'm just taking another glance to make sure I didn't miss anything."

Louie watched the first four races without making a bet. With two minutes left before the start of the fifth race Louie said, "I kinda like the 3-horse." Not exactly what I wanted to hear. I wanted him to say, "I *love* the 3-horse." Or, "The 3-horse is a *lock.*"

As the horses entered the starting gate, Louie called the race before the announcer said, "They're off."

His eyes were glued to his binoculars, and he spoke out of the side of his mouth. "She'll sit fourth or fifth until they hit the stretch and then she'll make her move. She'll go to the outside. If she gets boxed in, we're in trouble."

Louie was right. The horse ran the race just as he said she would. Some racing fans yell and scream and jump for joy when they have a winning horse. But not Louie. He laid his binoculars on the table, wrote something into his notebook, and went to the window to collect. The horse paid $7.

The second horse Louie liked was in the ninth race. It started to rain hard just as the sixth race went off. "Let's go," said Louie. "I don't like the weather conditions for my horse." That was it. We spent almost all day at the track. He bet one race.

In the car, Louie said, "I only bet a horse to win. No daily-doubles, no exotic bets. I never look for a price. That's the biggest mistake most horse players make. They've got the winner, but they don't like the price, so they bet another horse. Ninety-nine percent of the time they're giving up a winner because the price wasn't enticing enough. Your book is about casino gambling, right? So tell your readers that's why they lose in a casino. They're never satisfied with the price."

CHAPTER 2

Hidden Hooks: The Psychological Snare

Casino hooks are the subtle strategies that casinos use to change a player's behavior. A casino hook can turn even a disciplined player into an irresponsible loser. Without your knowing it, a casino hook can change the way you think. By learning to recognize and avoid casino hooks, you should become a stronger and smarter player.

Let me ask you a question. When you walk into a casino, what's the first thing you see? What do you hear and feel? The obvious answer is a crowded room with table games, ringing slot-machine bells, money, action, and excitement.

Twenty years ago I might have said the same thing. But after countless interviews with experienced dealers, casino managers, pit bosses, casino hosts, slot supervisors and attendants, floorpersons, and around-the-clock encounters with professional gamblers, I have a totally different perspective, a panoramic view, not from the player's side but from the casino's side.

What do I see when I walk through a casino? I see a statistical empire where, in the long run, every bet has been perfectly calculated to increase the casino's bottom line and separate the players from their money. But equally important, I see the traps that few other players see, so cleverly disguised but usually full of players. I jokingly refer to the traps as the "casino's catch of the day." And there's something else I hear... that seductive whisper of Lady Luck when a stickman says, "Pay the line," or a blackjack dealer says, "Dealer breaks." But exactly whose side is she on?!

Staying On Line

I was standing by the cashier's cage one night talking to a retired casino manager. His real name is Morris, but his friends call him "Gypsy." When Morris was a teenager, his dream was to play the guitar like the legendary jazz guitarist, Django Reinhardt. (Reinhardt was a Gypsy.) And so, at the tender age of 14, Morris became known as Gypsy. His dream came to an abrupt end when he broke his hand playing football.

Before his retirement, Gypsy spent 53 years working in casinos throughout Nevada. He started as a dealer and worked his way up to casino manager. Without a doubt he's probably forgotten more about gambling and the everyday operations of a casino than you and I could ever hope to learn in a lifetime. He's seen and done it all. He's a walking encyclopedia of casino stories.

As we were talking, I couldn't help but notice the long lines at the cashier's cage. Only two windows were open and the lines were moving very slowly. Players were getting edgy. Tempers were rising. No one was smiling. I said to Gypsy, "There's a big convention here tonight. Why don't they open more windows?"

"Stand here long enough," said Gypsy, "and you'll find out. Goodnight."

About five minutes later, I did. Players started leaving the line and going back to the tables! Instead of cashing in, they were *giving in* to their own lack of discipline. Is this an elusive "psychological" casino hook? A way of luring the player back to the tables? Or was it the new business trend of down-sizing payroll?

Out of curiosity, I walked over to the coin redemption booth, and guess what? The same thing was happening. There was a long line of players holding heavy coin buckets. One by one they went back to the machines.

The next night I told Gypsy what I thought. "Today, corporations run casinos the way IBM or AT&T run their businesses," said Gypsy, "your down-sizing theory might be right. But in the old days, we would close down windows on a busy night and players would instinctively go back to the tables. For most players, money does burn the proverbial hole in their pockets. A casino's main concern isn't what a player wins, it's what they leave behind."

Have you ever noticed the location of the cashier's cage and coin redemption booths? To get to the cashier's cage, you have to walk past the tables. To get to the coin redemption booth, you have to walk through a maze of slot machines. The temptation is to stop and play. After all, you're not broke. You have chips in your pocket or coins in a bucket. And that little voice in your head whispers, "What the hell, one more shot."

But let's say you have self-control and you walk straight to the cashier's cage and redeem your chips for cash. Well, you're only halfway home, because to get from the cashier's cage or coin redemption booth to your room, car, coffee shop, bathroom, cocktail lounge, showroom, buffet, gift shop, or exit, you have to walk past the tables and machines again.

Forget that little annoying voice in your head, trying to break you down. Now you have to fight The Almighty Voice: the casino's. It's a seductive voice. The temptress of Lady Luck. "Winner six. Pay the line." Keep walking. "Dealer breaks." Start jogging. Bells ring, wheels spin, people cheer, coins jingle and jangle as they pour out of slot machines. Start running. Are you strong enough to avoid the hook?

I discussed this with Gypsy one night, hoping he had a story. And leave it to Gypsy, he did. "When I was a casino manager, I never closed the tables by the cashier's cage even on a slow night. And I always told the stickman that every time the shooter made a pass, to say, 'Pay the line' as loud as he could. I also made sure that the slot machines by the redemption booths had a loud, piercing ring."

Gypsy told me a great story about a player he called, "Yo-Yo." No, he wasn't a toy manufacturer. But he was rich. Very rich.

"Yo-Yo was a *very* high roller," said Gypsy. "Yo-Yo had a million-dollar credit line and lost it all in four trips to Vegas. The first time I watched him play I knew how to hook him. His first love was baccarat and his mistress was craps.

"When I knew he was coming, I would rearrange the casino. I made sure that to get from the baccarat pit to the cashier's cage he would have to walk past rows of dice tables. One night he beat us for $250,000 playing baccarat. But on his way to the cashier's window, he stopped at every craps table and lost it all.

"He would ask for a marker, usually $200,000 or more, and go back to the baccarat pit and start all over again. This went on night after night. Baccarat pit, craps table, baccarat pit, craps table. Back and forth. Like a yo-yo. He never made it to the cashier's window once."

The Price Of Poker

Here's a hook everyone has felt. But it can backfire. Read how an Atlantic City casino manager describes his favorite ploy:

"On a busy night, we can control the player's betting pattern by raising the table-minimum bet. If you're a smart player, you should pick up your chips and leave. But casinos don't make million-dollar profits off smart players. We're betting that you'll stay and play. And so far, our bets have paid off handsomely."

Wait. There's more.

"After we periodically build up a loyal slot clientele, we phase out many of the quarter machines and replace them with half-dollar and dollar machines. We lure 'em in, then hit 'em with the bigger prices, and we do this for as long as we can before we have to bring out the quarter machines again."

So you think that's a shocker? It really isn't. Haven't you ever noticed the difference between a lunch menu and a dinner menu? That's right. Restaurants do this all the time! But getting back to casinos, here's a story where raising the prices really backfired:

A friend of mine who deals blackjack told me about a player who parlayed $500 into $53,000. "It was a $5 table when the guy sat down to play," said the dealer. "The player just kept winning bet after bet even though the other players at the table were losing. No matter what he did, he won! So we raised the minimum to $10. Even if he did something stupid like splitting tens, or doubling down on a hard 12, he won the hand. It was as if an angel was sitting on his shoulder and the devil on mine.

"After hours of play, the player's luck showed no sign of slowing down. We raised the table minimum to $25. The player kept on winning. We raised it to $50, then $100. The player's luck never wavered. I shuffled the cards after dealing a few hands even though no one suspected him to be a card-counter. That didn't work, either. They changed dealers. But luck and fate couldn't care less. Tonight, this player couldn't lose.

"The higher we raised the minimum the more the player won. Everything we did backfired on us. I've never seen that happen before. Raising the minimum bet on a winning player usually results in one thing: The player gives it all back... plus. But that night, the casino got a taste of its own medicine and, believe me, they had a hard time swallowing it."

A Family Affair

It wasn't too long ago when most people viewed gambling and casinos as a villainous vice. Casinos had the image of organized crime, prostitution, drunk gamblers blowing the rent money, cheating, and shady characters looking to con you out of your last dollar. The old stereotype image has been replaced with the "family friendly" theme.

Walk by a casino coffee shop and you'll probably see neatly dressed tourists holding a child in one hand and a videocam in the other. A retired casino manager told me, "This used to be a blood-and-guts gambling business. Players left the kids at home and came to gamble, period. Gambling isn't enough anymore. People are attracted by a casino's *theme*. And if they gamble, they forget about how much money they've lost because the theme is a gambling distraction. You get it? It's not an *a*ttraction, it's a *dis*traction! Pretty clever, huh!"

Casino advertising even has that *Good Housekeeping* seal-of-approval look: Wholesome as apple pie.

The moral: Don't let a casino's theme, particularly a "family" theme, seduce you into gambling. Don't let it blur the distinction between vacationing and gambling. Don't confuse Atlantic City with Orlando, or Las Vegas with Anaheim.

Playing For Comps

We talked about comps in the previous chapter, but there's more to be wary of.

For some casino players, a "comp" is like a status symbol. It's the brass ring for high rollers and the Cracker-Jack gift for the average player. Comps are the most effective casino hooks that have us all taking one more ride on the merry-go-round.

I'm sure you've heard the old saying, "There's no such thing as a free lunch." No other business in the world is more willing to give out free lunches, gourmet dinners, show tickets, rooms, suites, limo rides, travel expenses, and other amenities. All the casino asks in return is that you play, and play, and play, at its tables.

Let me assure you that any comp worth getting is strictly for the high roller. Would you like to stay in a 4,000 square foot European suite? I hope you have a credit line of at least $100,000. Perhaps you'd like your own private villa? Sure, that can be arranged if your credit line is over *two* hundred thousand dollars.

Professional gamblers never play for comps. They play for money. The casino's money. And that's the way the average player should play. A comp is nothing more than a casino pacifier! And every casino host has a favorite bedtime story:

"Better luck next time Mr. H. Don't worry about your room; it's taken care of. Goodnight and sleep well."

"After you signed that tenth marker I thought for sure your luck would change. Enjoy the lunch and champagne we have waiting for you in the limo."

"I've never seen cards come out of a shoe like that. We have a fine jewelry store here in the hotel. Go pick out something for your lovely wife."

Sometimes, though, you just can't give a comp away. Believe this story:

"There's this high roller who we call Charlie the Tuna," said Frank, a casino host in the Marina section of Atlantic City. "Charlie loves to fish and play blackjack, but not necessarily in that order. On his last trip here he wasn't catching any fish, but he sure was catching some cards. After two days he was up $85,000 but he still wasn't happy.

"Charlie was complaining about his bad fishing luck, saying that if he didn't catch any fish tomorrow he would leave. He was fishing for blue marlin. Now I know nothing about fishing. I'm from Brooklyn; fishing, for me, was driving over to Fulton's Fish Market on a Friday afternoon. But I knew I had to keep him here. So I told him to go 120 miles out to sea in a southwest direction.

"The following night Charlie's all smiles. He caught a thousand-pound marlin! The next day he caught another one. By this time, smiling Charlie lost the $85,000 plus another $65,000. I tried to give him a comp for dinner at the hotel's gourmet seafood restaurant, but Charlie wouldn't take it. He said, 'Thanks but no thanks. You see, I'm allergic to seafood!'"

Slot Comps

To qualify for a comp, you must be "rated," as we learned in the previous chapter. Slot players, the new breed of high rollers, can get rated, too. Rating a slot player is easy for a casino. Most slot players have a "player's card." Players insert the card in a box attached to the machine and, presto, their play is automatically recorded: Coins played, coins paid out, time played, and machine played. Rating a table player is personalized. Rating a slot player is computerized.

Slot players must avoid the same hooks that table players face. But there are two additional hooks that a slot player must avoid. The first one is the credit meter. If you win $10 or $25 at a table game, the dealer pays you immediately. Slot machines, however, now record your winnings as "credits." A credit meter camouflages the monetary value of a player's winnings. This is especially true for the quarter slot player. If the credit meter reads 400 credits, that's $100! Losing your credits doesn't seem nearly as bad as losing $100!

On a dollar or half-dollar machine, it's easier for players to calculate their credits into dollars. But notice that no machine ever shows a dollar-sign after the word *credit*.

The second hook for the slot player is going for the jackpot, regardless of the cost. The casino cleverly entices you with a jackpot in bold brilliant colors on the machine. You can't miss it. A slot player's approach to playing should be no different from a table player's: winning. Don't get me wrong, hitting a jackpot is great, but be realistic. Push that "cash out" button when you're ahead. Remember, it's money that's displayed on the meter. Not credits.

Tempo

Every game has a tempo of its own, but no casino game was meant to be a ballad. From the piped-in Muzak to the dealer's ability to keep the games moving, speed is not only the name of the game, it's the hook. Slowing up the games means slowing up the casino's profit. The faster the game... well, you fill in the blanks! Casinos may call the tunes, but only a smart player controls the tempo.

Most people are under the assumption that craps is the fastest game. But nothing beats the rapid pace of a slot machine. You press a button or pull a handle and in seconds you know the outcome. No one is rushing you to pull the handle or press the deal button. For slot players, the hook is their rush of adrenalin, their surge of anticipation, in the hope that the next pull is the jackpot. That next hand is the royal flush. That next hand is the sequential royal flush to end all royals! Wake up, dear slot player, and smell the coffee. Speed in the casino can be just as dangerous as on the highway. Don't let the casino set your speed limit. Play at your own pace.

If you want to see a fast-moving table game, watch a head-to-head $100-minimum blackjack game. High rollers usually like the fast pace. Dealers are quick to oblige. And casinos love it. Every dollar of it.

If the casino has an edge on nearly every hand (and it does) then it only stands to reason that the more hands dealt, the more profit for the casino. But there's more. There's a hook that few players think about. The dealers have only one decision to make: to hit until they have 17 or better. And if the dealers lose, it's not their money going down the drain.

But for the player, each hand is a challenge of decisions: hit, stand, split, double down, increase your bet, decrease your bet, take insurance, don't take insurance, stop playing, continue playing, move to another table. And after hours of fast-paced, non-stop action, your ability to make the *right* decisions starts to break down. I've seen some very good blackjack players fall apart under these conditions. On the other hand, I've seen some smart blackjack players take control of the game tempo and dance away with a nice profit.

There's only one game where both sides of the table usually agree on the tempo: craps. Everyone likes a smooth-running craps table. When the boxman, stickman, and dealers are all working together, the game just seems to flow. But when a shooter is making pass after pass, after pass, after pass, that's when the tempo changes. It's time for the hook.

Sometimes the casino uses a little reverse psychology. If the game is playing true to form, the casino will leave it alone. But when it's going against the grain, the casino wants to slow down the music.

The boxman may ask, "Is that your come-bet?" A few seconds tick by. The stickman fumbles with the dice before returning them to the shooter. A few more seconds pass. The shooter's rhythm is broken.

Suddenly, the boxman examines the dice. The shooter waits. The stickman is changed. The shooter waits. The shooter is warned about hitting the wall. The shooter waits. The game slows down like a car running out of gas. The whole tempo of the game starts to get choppy. Then—and these guys just seem to fall out of the sky— someone walks up to the table and scatters $1 prop-bets on all the hardways. This unknowing confederate has just come to the casino's aid. Such players slow down the game as if they were the casino's own shill. Regardless of how hard the shooter tries to restore the tempo, the inevitable happens: Loser seven is knocking at the door.

When Is A Win *Not* A Win?

The power of suggestion is alive and well when it comes to the paytables on video poker machines. For the sake of argument, let's say that you're playing a Jacks-or-Better quarter machine and wagering five coins per hand. The payout table posted on the machine reads: Jacks or Better, 5 coins. If you played five coins and got a pair of jacks, queens, kings or aces, the machine pays you five coins. Did you win? The word *WIN* flashes on the machine's screen and five coins are added to your credits. The machine is *suggesting* or *implying* that you've won. But the truth is, you simply broke even. In casino parlance, it's called a "push."

If you were playing blackjack and your hand totaled 20, and the dealer's hand totaled 20, the dealer doesn't say "Win." He knocks on the table and says, "Push." Don't be fooled into thinking that you've got a hot machine just because you're getting push after push. Any time a machine payoff matches your original bet, it's a push, not a win. Don't let the machine confuse or mislead you into thinking you're a winner. The only thing a push in video poker does is prolong the anxiety that the jackpot is a few hands away.

Parlay, Parlay, Parlay

FROM A LONG-TIME PIT BOSS: "In all my years, the most common mistake I've seen players make is parlaying their bets the minute they start to play. Blackjack and baccarat players are more likely than other table-game players to fall into this pattern of betting. They win the first hand and, boom, they parlay. If they win the next hand, they parlay again. They're going for the casino's jugular vein without any regard or respect for the game. I'm not talking about parlays when a table's hot, I'm talking right out of the chute. Gambling should not be about selfishness and greed. It should be about pacing and self-control. It's one hand at a time. Players aren't satisfied with a small win. So instead of walking to the cashier's cage with chips in their hands, they walk to the parking lot empty-handed.

"Sure, I could tell you a few isolated stories about the player who started out with a small bankroll and parlayed his way to a big win. But after 26 years of standing behind the tables, I can tell you thousands of stories that went the other way... the casino's way. Casinos love a parlay player because they know they've got a loser sitting at their table.

"Parlay players have no respect for a winning hand. They're under the impression that winning one hand is a signal that a hot streak is coming their way. Greed and a lack of betting discipline will only lead to a substantial loss for the player. You can't force a win. Trying to parlay small wins into large wins is like trying to climb a mountain taking reckless large steps instead of small cautious ones. Eventually, you'll slip and fall."

FROM AN EXPERIENCED BLACKJACK DEALER: "No player ever takes into account that winning three or four hands in a row is the exception, not the rule. If a $10 bettor parlayed three winning hands in a row and then lost the fourth hand, that player is giving back to the casino his winnings plus his original bet. In other words, he's down $80 and has to dig himself out of an $80 hole just to be even. Smart players should only increase their bets maybe 20 or 30 percent at a time. And change some red five-dollar chips for white one-dollar chips, if that's what it takes. Instead of pressing from five bucks to ten, bet seven dollars, so get some dollar chips to do it with. But more importantly, change your attitude.

"Day after day, we see players making mistakes that benefit the house. There is no such thing as a small mistake. These games are so hard to beat when played correctly that there's no room for error. Casino games are sensitive to the point that when players make insignificant mistakes, the game will immediately turn against them with a vengeance."

He's right. Some players make so many mistakes that, at times, I wonder if their biggest mistake was walking into a casino in the first place. From time to time, we all make gambling mistakes. It's almost unavoidable. We're humans, not computers. In his book *Conquering Casino Craps,* author John Gollehon wrote, "Those who say a casino is a microcosm of our lives are probably right. But more than anything else, the casino is a microcosm of our mistakes!"

A Rose By Any Other Name

Gambling in one form or another has spread across the country. The old speakeasy image of bust-out joints, shady characters, loaded dice, and marked cards is passé. The casino industry is now a "corporate" affair. The large corporations have given the casino industry a dose of respectability. They've also added a few new hooks.

The word *gambling* is no longer used. It's called *gaming*. But I never heard a player say, "I won $400 last night gaming!" Never forget that the minute you make a bet you are gambling. The word *gaming* only softens the blow.

Another hook is "player development." The term *player development* doesn't mean that the casino is trying to improve your playing skills or advance your knowledge of the games. Player development is a silent method of molding players to play the way the casino wants them to play.

Casinos never call a player a *loser*. Instead, they use the term *casino-oriented player*. Casino-oriented players usually have a large credit line, play longer than they should, play for comps, and have a betting strategy that favors the casino.

Players who start with small bets and only increase their size if they're winning are smart players, but not casino-oriented players.

In time, most casino-oriented players become desperate players. Helen, a pit boss, told me a story about one of them. "Fred is what we call a casino-oriented player.

He plays roulette for hours, making nothing smaller than $100 bets. One night he was down $9,500. He was so desperate to win that he left the table and called one of those 1-900 psychic lines. When he came back to the table, he looked confused. Do you know what the psychic told him his lucky number was? Thirty-seven!" (The highest number on a roulette wheel is 36.)

Gambling, like life, is a series of unpredictable events. No one knows with any certainty what the next draw of the card, toss of the dice, or spin of the wheel will be. And that's what makes gambling so exciting.

Uncertainty.

The anxiety of waiting to find out if you win or lose.

It's the biggest hook of all.

CHAPTER 3

Getting Even:
The Hook Players
Set Themselves

What's the biggest lie heard in the casino? "I'm about even!" If everyone were "about even," casinos throughout the country would be out of business. Truth is, a lot of players are losers... and liars.

Casino profits are not generated by players who are "about even." The foundation of a casino's bottom line is built by all the players *trying* to get even. Chasing lost money is like walking on quicksand. The more you try to wiggle your way out, the faster and deeper you sink. No one would build a $500 million casino if gambling were a break-even business.

"The toughest battle you can face in the casino is trying to recoup your losses," said a pit boss named Lori. "When players start to increase their bets thinking that their luck will change, the roof usually falls in on them. The smartest thing to do is to walk. If you can't leave the table, at least reduce your bet size. If you want to be a successful player, never chase a losing streak."

I'm sure you've heard the old saying, "Don't get mad, get even." But the truth of the matter is that when players lose, they get mad. And anger is one emotion that can turn a sensible player into a foolish player. For some players, losing their temper in a casino has cost them more than money.

I remember seeing a blackjack player punch the table after the dealer drew five cards for a total of 21. The player literally broke his hand. No, he wasn't betting $1,000 a hand. He was betting $5.

A change person told me a hard-to-believe story about a video poker player. I'll just give you the punch line: "This woman kept missing the royal flush by one card. I mean, ONE card! I bet it happened half a dozen times. She became so enraged that she started banging her head against the machine until she knocked herself out cold!"

Here's another believe-it-or-not:

A craps shooter was playing alone at a $100-minimum table. Down $26,000, he picked up the dice, tossed them in his mouth, and tried to swallow them. They lodged in his throat, choking him, until a quick-thinking pit boss performed the Heimlich Maneuver, thus saving the frustrated craps shooter's life.

On the lighter side, there's a funny story about comedian Shecky Greene. He was shooting craps one night and losing. In frustration, he jumped on the craps table, laid his body over the green felt, and said, "I bet my life!"

A professional gambler once told me, "For a gambler, every day is judgment day. If you win, it's heaven. If you lose, it's hell. And if you break even, it's purgatory. Judging from what I see in the casino, a few players go to heaven, hell is over-crowded, and purgatory is a ghost town."

No one wants to be a loser. Losing hurts our pride and destroys our confidence. But losing can also teach us something about ourselves as players and people. "Learn by your mistakes," a wise man once said. I firmly believe that if you want to celebrate the thrill of victory you must experience the agony of defeat.

"I've learned more about gambling from my losing sessions," said a professional gambler, "than from my winning sessions. Losing has taught me to respect the game and to never take winning for granted. If you're going to gamble, having a losing night, week, or month is unavoidable. It's a fact of life that all players should be aware of. For me, it's not how much I win, it's knowing when to walk away. I have a very strict loss limit. Taking out more money, hoping to get even on a losing night is like throwing gasoline on a burning fire.

You can't fight a losing streak. It'll knock you on your ass every time!"

Few players have a realistic approach about gambling or winning. They dream of the big score, the "bail out" bet. They have what I call "a lottery mentality"—a small bankroll and a million-dollar dream. Spare yourself the nightmare and put things in perspective. If you go to a casino with $100, $500, $1,000, $10,000, $100,000 or even a million dollars in your pocket, don't expect to walk out with the license on the wall.

Most players don't realize that winning is *not* the hardest thing to do in a casino. The hardest thing to do in a casino is to leave with your winnings in your pocket! The second hardest thing is accepting a losing night.

Desperadoes

There is one particular casino host whom I consider a close friend. She's very secretive about her professional life and wishes to remain anonymous. Let's call her "Irene." Irene's retired now, but in her day she had a little black book of player's names that was the envy of every casino host in the business... millionaires from Europe, Asia, South America, and the United States. She called it her "book of whales." (*Whales* is a term casinos use to identify the highest of their high rollers.)

One night I met Irene in a casino coffee shop. As usual, we started talking about gamblers and the casino business. I told her I was writing a chapter about getting even.

Smiling, Irene said, "When Vegas was this country's
only gambling destination, Sunday afternoons became
getting-even day. Or as one pit boss called it, 'Monday
night football on a Sunday afternoon.' After two or three
days, 99 percent of my junket players were losers. And
no one wants to go home a loser. They were all in a
hurry to get even and catch their flights. The $1,000-a-
hand baccarat player starts betting $3,000 a hand and
parlaying every win hoping to catch a hot streak."

"It's like the two-dollar horse player," I said, "who
hasn't picked a winner all night. Now it's the last race,
and suddenly he's betting $100 across the board."

"Exactly," said Irene. "Players become desperadoes.
Get even no matter what the cost. And most of the time
the cost is very, very high. Some players act as if they're
on death row waiting to be executed. Every minute and
every hand is life or death. Casinos will outlive all of
us. So what's the hurry? If you're not mature enough to
take a loss, don't play. Very few players will go to
their graves even. But by that time, who the hell cares?"

Irene told me about a craps player from New York.
A stickman nicknamed him "The Babe" because the
player looked like Babe Ruth. His play matched his
size: $1,000 pass-line and come-bets with full odds, $500
hardways, $100 elevens.

One night, Babe was throwing number after number,
pass after pass, back-to-back hardways. "The Babe left
the table with $78,000," said Irene. "Later that night
I'm walking through the cocktail lounge and I see Babe
sitting all alone. He looked sad sitting there nursing a

drink. I asked him if he needed anything. He turned to me and said, 'Irene, if I had only held the dice for another 20 minutes I would have been even for the weekend.'"

Downbeat

There's a great getting-even story about the renowned trumpet player and band leader, Harry James. For those of you who aren't familiar with Harry's playing, watch the movie *Young Man With A Horn* starring Kirk Douglas. Harry James did all the trumpet playing. A friend of mine who played in Harry's band for ten years told me this story:

"Harry loved wine, women, song, and keno. But not necessarily in that order. We were playing in Reno," said Harry's ex-sideman. "Harry used to slouch down when he was playing. A lot of young trumpet players thought he did this to get a breath. But the truth was that Harry was bending down to get a look at the keno board across the room.

"So one night Harry's playing this beautiful solo on "I Can't Get Started." He slouches lower and lower and then he stops playing. Turning his back to the audience and looking straight at the band he said, 'I just hit for $25,000. Three more hits like that and I'm even!' Harry, may he rest in peace, never did get even."

You might find it hard to relate to the dollar values in these two stories. But the amount of money involved is all relative. For some players, a $500 loss can be devastating. For others, it might be a six-figure loss. Losing not only affects your bankroll but it also destroys your ability to think clearly. Losing makes players vulnerable and weakens their ability to deal with the emotional stress that inevitably comes as the after-shock of a losing session. They feel rejected and lonely. Ego and greed affect the way they play and bet. Getting even, no matter what the cost, becomes an obsession, a very expensive obsession. This is when a $500 loss can escalate into an $800 or $1,000 loss. Don't dig yourself into a hole and then shovel the dirt in on top of you.

The reality of gambling is simple. Players will experience hot and cold streaks. It's like the old joke about two guys who meet in the casino. The first guy says, "So how are you doing, Joe?" "It's the same old story," says Joe. "One day I win. One day I lose." Joe's friend thinks for a minute and says, "Why don't you gamble every other day?"

Casinos accept the fact that players will have winning sessions. There will always be the occasional hot hand at a craps table or a big slot-machine payout. But the real bet the casino is making is that no player can win with any consistency. Smart players know how to make a hot streak turn into a volcano. They also know how to survive a cold streak without freezing to death. In other words, if you're having a losing session, don't try to play catch-up by losing your shirt. In life, patience is a virtue. In a casino, patience is imperative. And unless you're built like Fabio or Dolly Parton, I'm sure no one wants to see you with your shirt off!

For sports bettors, the biggest getting-even day of the year is Super Bowl Sunday. That's the day when most football bettors take their last shot at getting even for the season. Sports bettors look at this game the same way casino players look at their final day of a weekend trip to a casino. Bet big. Throw caution to the wind. Get even.

Every year the amount of money bet on Super Bowl Sunday escalates. Last year, $78 million was bet legally and $5 *billion* was bet *il*-legally. These figures tell me two things: (1) Sports bettors are just as obsessed with getting even as the casino player, and (2) bookies cash in on Super Bowl Sunday.

Truth Or Consequences

Some people self-destruct in a casino. Are you one of them? Answer the following questions:

(1) Have you ever turned a winning session into a losing one?

(2) If you lose, do you blame the dealers or other players?

(3) If you lose, do you feel lonely and rejected?

(4) Do you anticipate a loss the minute you set foot in a casino?

(5) When you run out of money, do you go to an ATM or credit-card machine?

I hope you answered NO to every question. If you didn't, it's time for you to examine not only how you play, but *why* you play. What separates the typical weekend player from the serious player is motivation and discipline. Weekend players, skilled or unskilled, have no realistic plan to win. They typically play for the fun and excitement that casinos happily provide. The serious player is motivated to *win*. Winning is fun. I've never seen losers laughing, no matter how much "fun" they said they had!

Did You Really Win?

How many times has this happened to you? You just returned home from a long weekend of gambling and the phone rings. It's your friend Nosey Body. The first words out of Nosey Body's mouth are, "So how did you do?"

There are four ways you can answer that question: (1) I won, (2) I lost, (3) I'm about even, or (4) you can dance around the truth until the music stops playing.

To illustrate the meaning of answer No. 4, I would like to borrow a story from John Gollehon's bestseller, *Conquering Casino Craps:*

Marty just got back from Vegas and he's telling his friend about his big score at the craps table on his first night in town. "The shooter held the dice for 40 minutes," says Marty. "I walked away with ten grand!"

"Great," says Marty's friend. "But how did you do for the trip?"

Marty is not paying attention and rambles on. "The next morning I hit 'em for another $3,000."

Again his friend says, "Yeah, but how did you do for the trip?" There's a pause in the conversation. "I gave a little back," says Marty, whispering.

"How much back?"

"Oh, I don't know." All the excitement in Marty's voice is gone.

"Marty, how did you do for the trip?"

"Umm, I... I lost a few thousand."

This story is the classic example of how thousands of players react when asked the question: How did you do? Never kid yourself into thinking you won when you really lost. Don't let an isolated win blind you from seeing the bottom line.

Business Or Pleasure

Casinos sell gambling. That's their product. They advertise gambling as "entertainment." That's their way of saying, "Count your losses as the cost of being entertained." Let's put things into perspective. If you want to be entertained, go see a show or a casino lounge act. I really doubt that players in their right mind think that losing money is entertaining.

The Smartest Player I Know

I love hanging out in casinos. Over the years I've met some very interesting and colorful characters. Professional gamblers, con men, hustlers, millionaires, and celebrities. But the smartest player I ever met is none of the above. He's just an average married guy with two kids, a dog, a mortgage, and a car payment. He isn't a card-counter or dice mechanic; and by no means is he a high roller. But he is the most disciplined player I've ever met.

"It all started with a $500 Christmas bonus," said Phil, who lives 20 minutes away from a casino. "Like most people today, my wife and I live on a tight budget. I was looking for a way to lessen my $250-a-month car payment by $100. And that's when I came up with this idea."

Phil's idea was simple. Let small wins accumulate and never lose more than $30 a day. With a $500 bankroll to work with, Phil would walk over to a craps table and buy in for $30. He'd bet $10 on the pass-line. If the shooter rolled a 7 or 11 on the come-out, Phil picked up his $10 profit and left the casino. If the shooter threw a craps on the come-out, he accepted the $10 loss and walked away. But if the shooter established a point, Phil would back up his bet with double odds, $20.

"At this point," said Phil, "I'd have one foot out the door. If the shooter sevens out, I leave because that's my $30 loss for the day. If the shooter made his point, I'd pick up the money and run. When I reached my monthly target of $100, I'd stop playing until the next four-week cycle began."

Phil kept a journal and recorded his monthly bottom line. After 12 months he showed a profit of $1,000. I asked Phil if he had ever walked away from a hot table. "Twice," said Phil, "but I don't dwell on it, because I walked away from hundreds of cold tables after making my little profit for the day. Everyone dreams about the hot table and occasionally it happens. But how many nights of cold tables proceeded that hot one? I'm a hit-and-run player. It's strictly dollars and cents to me. In fact, I don't really enjoy playing!"

Happy motoring, Phil.

The Color Of Money

Something funny happened last night that I must tell you about before I close this chapter. A friend of mine, who grew up in the city, married a girl from Nebraska. They decided to spend part of their honeymoon in Atlantic City. She was raised on a farm and had never been in a casino until last night. My friend taught her how to play blackjack. She had the basic strategy memorized but wanted to watch her husband play for a while just to get the feel of the game. He was betting green chips. "How much are those chips?" his wife asked.

"A quarter each," said my friend. After a few hands, his beeper started beeping and he had to leave the table to make a call. Before he left the table, he turned to his wife and said, "You play for a while."

She started betting one, then two chips a hand. She was winning and began increasing her bets to four, five, and sometimes eight chips a hand. Beginner's luck was certainly living up to its name. Three shoes later my friend returned. His eyes opened wide when he saw the stacks of chips in front of his wife.

"It's seven o'clock," said my friend. "Why don't we go have dinner?"

We all helped carry the chips to the cashier's window. The cashier counted the chips twice and said, "That's $7,800."

My friend's wife said, "Excuse me?!"

"Seven thousand, eight hundred dollars," answered the cashier.

The newlywed looked at her husband and said, "I thought you said that each chip was a quarter."

"That's right. Twenty-five dollars each. A quarter of a hundred. They're called 'quarters' for short."

"Are you crazy?!" she said. "Betting that kind of money. If I knew that..."

I walked away because I got the feeling the honeymoon was over!

CHAPTER 4

Slot Players Beware!

"Forty years ago, the main function of a slot machine was to give women something to do while they waited for their husbands to run out of cash at our table games," said a veteran casino manager. "A slot machine used to be a simple device: Pull down the arm, and spinning reels with pictures of fruit would spin by. Today, slot machines have reached a new level of savoir-faire by offering the player a multitude of betting options, CD-quality sound, bonus jackpots, elaborate graphics, and other features that keep a player interested enough to sit there for hours at a time. The days of seeing those bored handle-pullers are over."

Slot machines have gone through periods of boom and bust. The big rise in slot play started in 1986 when

Megabucks was introduced. The jackpot started at $1 million and grew to $5 million in less than one year. Terry Williams was the first player to hit a Megabucks jackpot at Harrah's in Reno, Nevada. He won $4,988,842.14.

Today, casino analysts call slot machines "high-tech cash cows." On Indian reservations and riverboats, from the Vegas Strip and along the Atlantic City Boardwalk, slot machines are outpacing earnings from table games.

"The look and feel of a casino has changed," said a casino host. "I can remember the days when table games dominated this business and slot machines were trivial. But that's no longer the case. For better or worse, casinos are starting to look and sound like video arcades."

The days of the small, three-reel slot machines are over. High-tech slot machines are, without a doubt, the wave of the future. Recently, at the World Gaming Congress & Expo, the industry's largest international conference and trade show, manufacturers unveiled their newest machines. The new spin on slots (pardon the pun) is designed to entertain the players as they pour quarter after quarter into these state-of-the-art coin guzzlers.

Touch-screen video games and slots with dueling race cars and pinball games on top will certainly attract the younger generation. But will the Social Security community, who dominate the slot market, be turned off by these high-tech, computer-style machines? "Players will flock to any new product we put out on the floor," said one senior vice president of slot operations, "even the little old ladies."

Soon, you'll be able to watch your favorite television show without leaving your machine. Cable-ready slot machines are coming to a casino near you. The whole concept behind this new evolution in slot machine design seems to focus on the player's need to be entertained. "It's elementary," said one casino marketing executive, "win or lose, players want to have fun. When the *Wheel of Fortune* machines hit the market, they were an overnight success. Players weren't interested in the odds or percentage of payback. They wanted to have fun."

Based on the success of its *Wheel of Fortune* machines, IGT has developed a *Jeopardy* slot machine. Drop a few coins into the machines and you'll hear Johnny Gilbert say, "This is Jeopardy!" All these new concept machines are designed to make you play longer without boring you to death.

Hiding The Percentages

"We've seen a drastic change in how we market slot play," said a Lake Tahoe slot host. "Players used to put money in a machine and their only concern was winning or losing. But today, they want to be entertained. If we can give slot players entertainment value for their dollar, I guarantee you that we'll have a steady slot customer. Anytime we put new machines on the floor, players stand in line to try them. It's money in the bank for us because we can hide the percentages. That's why some casinos have fewer video poker machines. On a video poker machine we can't hide the percentages."

Here's another casino executive to confirm this: **"The only slot players who *read* and *understand* the payout percentages are the astute video poker players.** Unlike the regular slot players, the smart video poker players compare the payout per coin on a machine before they play. Regular slot players just walk aimlessly around the casino, going from one machine to another. A good video poker player doesn't play if the machine's paytables lean too much in favor of the house."

One night I overheard a lady asking a slot attendant where the 6-9 video poker machines were. The attendant had no idea what the lady was talking about. "All I see are 5-8 machines," said the frustrated player. "And I refuse to play them." From overhearing this conversation I knew that the lady was a serious video poker player and the slot attendant should have been working someplace else.

The difference is well worth looking for. Let's use a 25-cent poker machine as an example. The difference between the 6-9 and the 5-8 machines refers to the payout per coin played for a flush and full house. If you're playing the 5-coin maximum, a 6-9 machine will pay $7.50 for a flush and $11.25 for a full house. On a 5-8 machine, a flush pays $6.25 and a full house only pays $10.00.

It doesn't sound like much until you think about *extended play*, in other words, long term. And your only concern should be the long term.

If, for example, you were playing a 6-9 machine and after days of play you got 100 flushes, ($750) and 100 full houses ($1,125), you would have made $1,875. Now let's compare those figures to a 5-8 machine, 100 flushes is $625, and 100 full houses is $1,000, making a total of $1,625. If you were playing the 5-8 machine, you gave away $250 in winnings back to the house.

"Years ago, players never complained about the lack of 6-9 machines," said one slot executive. "But now that players are becoming more knowledgeable, they are demanding better odds. We're getting fewer players on our 5-6 machines; most of the play is on our bank of 5-8s. We don't have 6-9s like you find in Nevada."

More On Video Poker

In recent years, video poker has become one of the most popular games in the casino. Its rapid rise in popularity has overwhelmed casino insiders. Unlike regular slot machines, video poker combines skill and luck. The player has choices to make on every hand, which, in turn, gives the player a feeling of power and control over the machine.

To trace the history of poker machines, we have to go back to 1890. In the days following the Gold Rush, gambling was flourishing in the San Francisco Bay area. Poker machines could be found in the rowdy bars that

catered to the so-called rough-neck crowd. The jackpots were paid in "trade checks," not cash. A player
hitting a royal flush could get 100 free cigars or drinks.
In 1909, the San Francisco Board of Supervisors out-
lawed slots because players almost always came out on
the short end. They estimated that the 3,200 illegal machines were grossing $12 million annually.

The more things change, the more they remain the
same. In 1997, a North Carolina judge ruled that video
poker games are illegal because players have virtually
no chance to win. The judge fined a Dunn, North Carolina businessman $1,000. Prosecutors set up four video
poker machines in the courtroom and demonstrated how
fast players could lose their money. "The payoff
percentages," said the judge, "are programmed in the
machines, and no amount of skill can change those percentages."

Here's what my publisher, John Gollehon, who has
authored several books on gaming, has to say about this
rather unusual ruling. "When a video poker machine
manufacturer sets the percentages, whether it's 92 percent or 99 percent, or whatever percentage, it's usually
based on what is called *optimum play*. And that means
applying the maximum level of skill. So, over the long
haul, the judge is probably right that no level of skill
will defeat the percentages. Well, duh!

"A player's best chance of winning is obviously in
the short term. But short-term play leads to long-term
exposure. The best advice is to keep your playing sessions short and sweet."

Now, let's listen in as a Nevada casino executive puts in *his* nickel's worth. "Every month, in various casino trade publications, you can read about a casino's revenue from table games and slot machines. Occasionally you might see a drop in table revenue resulting from the odds shifting to the other side of the table. Believe it or not, it happens from time to time. But slot revenues never waver from players getting lucky. Knowing this, I can't think of one substantial reason why anyone would spend the time and money playing a slot machine. But, fortunately for us, they do."

Fortunately for slot players, Gollehon refutes that statement: "To take the edge off this executive's rather damning opinion of slot players, let me tell you that the revenue-generating characteristics of slot machines only *seems* unwavering to him because of the multitude of machines in a typical sampling. Some casinos have literally thousands of machines. Obviously, there are far fewer table games, so greater fluctuations in win revenue at the tables should be expected. If only a relatively few slot machines were monitored for revenue performance, as would be the case with table games, I can assure you the machines would 'waver.' All slot players know that a machine produces 'ups and downs.' But they also know that there are more 'downs' than 'ups,' particularly over extended play. At the risk of repeating myself, the trick is to limit your play, try to catch a nice ride up, and when it's over, get off!"

Popular Slots

Slot enthusiasts are unpredictable. A popular machine model one day can became a dust collector the next. I say this because, as I write this chapter, things may change. I conducted a recent survey to find out what slot machine models are the most preferred by players. According to the slot executives I spoke to, Double Diamond machines in Colorado, Atlantic City, and areas in the South and Midwest get the most play.

In East Peoria, Illinois, at the Par-A-Dice Riverboat Casino, the Double Diamond and the Fourth-of-July machines are the player's choice. The majority of players at the Par-A-Dice Riverboat are women who are 55-plus years of age. According to a vice-president I spoke to, "The Double Diamond lends itself well to our average customer. The color scheme and the diamonds in the artwork are geared toward the female senior, our primary customers."

Another machine, called Red, White and Blue, is hot right now, especially in southern Nevada and on cruise ships. RWB also has a large share of the Native American market.

Most slot hosts believe that, over the years, players have become more knowledgeable about slots. Players still may take a shot at hitting Megabucks or Quartermania, but most of their play is for smaller jackpots. They want to play machines that give them more play for their buck.

In Mississippi, there are more than 300 Megabucks machines in 30 casinos throughout the state. When the starting point for the system's top jackpot rose from $1 million to $3 million, the popularity of the machine grew even greater. The Double Diamond games at the Grand Casinos in Biloxi and Gulfport, Mississippi, get more play than video poker. (Mississippi now has more gambling square footage than Atlantic City. Its 29 casinos contain 1.3 million square feet, compared with 1.2 million square feet for Atlantic City's 13 casinos.)

The Double Diamond and Red, White and Blue machines may not be the most popular machines in every casino throughout the country. In Minnesota, it's Caribbean Gold. At Sam's Town in Las Vegas, Double Bonus Poker is the most popular game.

In some gambling jurisdictions where players stay for two or three days, staying power is their main concern. "Players want their gambling budget to last," said one president of slot operations. "These customers are paying for playing time. So payout percentage and hit frequency are two very important elements for slot machine play to remain popular."

A designer who developed slot models for Bally's Manufacturing told me that the Blazing 7s were designed to have frequent winners in the 100- to 300-coin range.

I remember when Bally's came out with Black Gold. The $5 machine debuted at a time when the industry was lacking a specifically designed machine for the $5 player. The interesting thing to me was that many of the payouts were just under $1,200, which eliminated the paperwork (W2-G) required by the government for jackpots over that amount.

Traps And Tidings

FROM A RENO SLOT SUPERVISOR: "The term we use is *extended play*. It's the secret to expanding our slot revenue. I hate to see a player sitting at a machine that has a malfunction. When a play stoppage occurs, that's lost revenue for the casino. On a busy night I tell my attendants to pay off jackpots as soon as possible because I don't want the player to sit there thinking. I don't want to give the player the time to think about doing something other than playing.

"But on a slow night, having the player wait for an attendant isn't a bad idea. Why? Because when the casino is slow, the machine next to the player waiting for an attendant is usually empty. And 99 percent of the time that player will start playing that empty machine just to pass the time until an attendant pays off that player's jackpot. We get some of that jackpot money back just by stalling for time."

FROM A CONNECTICUT SLOT HOST: "Without a doubt, slot machines have become the most popular form of casino gambling in America. People read about someone hitting a $6 million MEGABUCKS jackpot and they think to themselves, *Boy, would that solve all my problems*. Casinos love a press release like that."

For a game to be successful, it must fill a void. Casinos needed a simple game that anyone can play. They needed to create a game for people who know nothing about table games and feel embarrassed to sit at a table surrounded by experienced players. Slot machines fill that void by offering a player privacy. It's player against machine. The player controls the pace, and the intimidation factor of making a dumb play does not exist. The icing on the cake that lures more and more players to these electro-mechanical machines are the larger-than-life progressive jackpots.

FROM A MINNESOTA SLOT SUPERVISOR: "From the casino's viewpoint, the real beauty of slot machines is economics. They work 24 hours a day, 365 days a year. There are no health benefits, pensions, sick days, or salary increases to worry about. When I walk past a bank of slot machines, I don't see machines. I see row after row of casino piggy-banks swallowing up coins and driving up the casino's profit margin."

Less than two years after Delaware allowed slot machine play at its racetracks, the state's share from slot revenue was $91 million. Delaware House Majority Leader Wayne Smith said, "There is no doubt about it. We're drunk on the revenues."

Cheers, Wayne.

FROM A LAS VEGAS SLOT DESIGNER: "The player has absolutely no control over the odds that are programmed into any machine. Legitimate casinos do not rig their slot machines, because, by doing so, they have everything to lose and nothing to gain. In Nevada, the Gaming Commission and Gaming Control Board are responsible for licensing and regulating all of the gaming activities. Major corporations that invest millions and millions of dollars to build a casino are not going to jeopardize their gaming license just to cheat the player out of a few quarters."

The only people cheating are the players. Each year Nevada casinos lose $20 million to cheaters. In a five-year period, Nevada gaming officials investigated over 12,000 cases of slot cheating. If caught and convicted, slot cheaters in Nevada could be fined from $25,000 to triple the amount of their cheating gains. They could also spend five to 20 years in prison.

FROM A LAUGHLIN, NEVADA SLOT HOST: "The biggest psychological trap we set for slot players is getting them into a 'jackpot mentality.' In other words, any win shy of the jackpot just won't do. The casino is setting the player's goal, not the player. Most slot players take the 100- or 200-coin hits and play them off. Players aren't satisfied unless they hit the jackpot. It's that all-or-nothing attitude that drives up our bottom line."

FROM A MISSISSIPPI CASINO EXECUTIVE: "Players have a misconception about the hold percentage on slot machines. If the machine is set to hold six percent from the player, some players think that they can only lose six percent of all the coins they play. The six percent hold isn't based on short-term play. Anything can happen in the short term. Like table games, the percentages for slot machines are based on long-term play."

It wasn't that long ago when most slot machines looked alike. But computer technology has paved the way for casinos to offer the player a wide variety of machines. The old reels and gears have been replaced by microchips.

Today, theme slot machines are in vogue. Most people think that this trend started in the '80s, but they're wrong.

The first person who introduced the concept of "theme" slot machines was Bill Harrah. Bill Harrah's first casino opened over 50 years ago in Reno, Nevada. To be different from the other casinos, Harrah used a sultan, or genie, on the front of each machine. Harrah's slot machine action was enormous. The success of Harrah's slot revenue puzzled everyone, except Bill Harrah.

According to Harrah's, "The other casinos tried to duplicate it, but they couldn't. They tried to copy the sultan, but they couldn't. They'd try to tighten up their slots, but that didn't work, because while they were tightening, they were missing Bill Harrah's big secret. He was *loosening* his slots, and counting on the volume to give him the profits, and that worked like a charm."

FROM A LAKE TAHOE CASINO MANAGER: "Years ago, so-called serious gamblers and casino executives laughed at video poker players, calling them 'the clowns' in the casino. Today, video poker players are considered serious gamblers and constitute a large share of a casino's high roller market. The only clowns in this industry are the people who design, market, and fill the casinos with poker machines. You'll never see them frown."

The old style reel-to-reel machines are slowly fading away. Games like Jacks or Better, Joker Poker, Double Jokers, and Deuces Wild, are beginning to dominate the slot market. All slot machines, including video poker, were designed to pay back a lesser percentage of what goes in. Short-term play can't be the measure. However, in the short term, anything can happen. But in the long term, the machine will approach its hold percentage, giving the casino its unwavering edge over the player.

The most comprehensive book on video poker was written by Dwight and Louise Crevelt. The title of the book is *Video Poker Mania*, a must-read for anyone who plays video poker. They write in great detail about a machine cycle of 2,598,960—the number of different 5-card hands you can be dealt. The authors also say that to have a 91 percent chance of hitting a royal flush you would have to play about 100,000 hands! I never heard a slot host, supervisor, or attendant tell that to a player. They also won't tell you that video poker is very addictive.

Loose Goose

We've all read casino advertisements proclaiming the "loosest" slot machines in town. Some casinos might even boast that their machines have a 99.9 percent payout rate. But don't be misled. *Loose*, like the word *gaming,* are casino-industry slang words. A so-called loose machine doesn't mean that the casino is guaranteeing you a winning session.

Built into all computerized machines is something called the Random Number Generator that is constantly sending out combinations of reel-symbols every microsecond. The RNG also calculates the number of pulls and coins played. Over time, the machine will pay back a precise percentage to the players. Because of this device, no one can predict when a machine is "due" to hit.

If you've been staying up nights trying to come up with a system to beat the slots, don't waste your time. Don't be under the misconception that a machine is "overdue" or "ready for a payoff." Hitting a slot jackpot is sheer luck. Random games produce random results.

Down-sizing

There was a time when slot players didn't have to leave their machine to get change. All the player had to do was press the change button. The little light on top of the machine would catch the attention of a change attendant and he or she would push the cart right over to your machine and, presto, 40 quarters for a ten dollar bill. Over the past years I've noticed a reduction in change personnel in most casinos.

I asked numerous slot supervisors about the apparent lack of change attendants and the reduction of change booths. The standard answer was, "The casino is downsizing its payroll. We've replaced the change booths with slot machines. Machines generate profits; change booths don't."

Sometimes the standard answer isn't the "right" answer. No one gets rich by being a change attendant. And a change booth does not take away a substantial amount of floor space. After spending endless hours standing around watching slot players hop from machine to machine, the "right" answer became apparent. When players "feed" coins into a machine, they seem to hit and run. But when a player inserts cash into a machine, 99 percent of the time that player will play the credit meter down to zero.

If you're holding a bucketful of coins in your hands, you can feel the value of your money increase or decrease. But when you look at a credit meter, your perception of actual "money value" becomes distorted.

Let's say that you're tired and it's been a bad night for you at the machines but you feel like taking one more shot. You sit down at a quarter Jokers Wild video poker machine and reach into your pocket for some money. All you have are three twenty-dollar bills. Because you've been losing, you only want to play $10.

Do you get up and walk to the cashier's window for change? The few change attendants on duty who now carry cash instead of coins are nowhere to be found. If you insert the twenty-dollar bill into the machine, will you have the discipline to push the cash-out button when the credit meter reads 40 credits?

The casino doesn't think so. In fact, it's betting that you don't. Don't fall into this trap. If slots are your game, get change at the coin redemption booth *before* you sit down to play. Or change your large bills for smaller ones. Never let a casino influence your betting strategy.

According to most slot executives I've talked to, the next phase for slot players will be the use of major credit cards. The technology is already in place. In other words, the trap is set. All that the players will have to do is insert their Visa or Master Card into the machine and "charge" their play on their credit card. When and if this happens, I'm sure that the casinos will say that this is a convenience for the player. When, in reality, it's just another way to get you to play more without actually using cash or coins.

Cash-Back Programs

Slot clubs have revolutionized the casino industry. Most slot clubs have a cash-back policy. When a player inserts his or her slot card into a machine, a computer system will record the amount of coins played, plus time spent at that machine. The computerized slot-rating system can identify and evaluate a player's action to the penny. Some casinos will mail the player a coin-voucher. The amount of that voucher is based solely on play. Casinos are shying away from words like *cash-rebate*, or *merchandise giveaways*. The new term is *reward*.

Is this so-called "cash reward" system good for the player or the casino? Why are casinos so willing to give cash back to slot players?

FROM AN ATLANTIC CITY SLOT EXECUTIVE: "Cash-reward programs have been very successful for us. When we mail a cash-reward voucher to a player, it accomplishes two things: (1) The player has to return to our casino to cash in his reward, and (2) he'll play back the reward money and more. We send him another cash reward and the cycle goes on and on."

This response reminds me of a great story about an old casino manager who would walk around his casino handing out rolls of quarters to slot players. Someone once asked him why he was giving away money. "Do you think I'm giving away money?" said the casino manager. "All I'm giving the players is a little extra time."

What's Wrong With This Picture?

I was walking through a casino one night with a friend of mine who's the casino manager. It was a holiday weekend, and the casino was very busy. As we walked past a bank of slot machines, our path was suddenly blocked by a crowd of onlookers standing by a jackpot-ringing slot machine. With no room to move, we stood there watching the excitement.

The casino manager was eyeing the crowd for a few seconds before he said, "As soon as these bells and buzzers go off everyone comes over to the machine and looks at the winning player sitting there. Whether they're jealous, happy, or whatever, the winner becomes their focus. They should really be looking around at all the *other* people who *didn't* win. That's the reality no one pays attention to."

CHAPTER 5

A Word From The Wise: Tips From The Insiders

Research for this book gave me the opportunity to talk with the casino industry's *insiders:* CEOs, casino managers, shift and pit bosses, floorpersons, dealers, and slot supervisors. I prodded them to reveal some valuable tips that could be beneficial to all players. From the quarter slot player to the $5,000-per-hand baccarat player, there's something in this chapter for everyone.

The insiders who watch us play see our strengths and weaknesses. They watch us win. They watch us lose. They see players constantly making the same mistakes over and over. No one knows what will happen when you pull the arm of a slot machine or toss a pair of dice across a craps table. There is always risk, but knowing how to play smart can reduce the risk factor. Hopefully, the information in this chapter will help you become a smarter player.

Believe it or not, casino bosses have told me that they see more mistakes at the slot machines than at any other game. Most of the tips in this chapter will deal directly with slot machines. From the players to the paytables, these off-the-cuff tips will improve your playing skills and teach you which machines to avoid.

One day a casino executive was giving me a grand tour of a newly built slot section. "We now have an additional 500 slot machines on our casino floor," he proudly stated. We stopped walking for a moment and took in the sights and sounds. Then, out of the clear blue sky he casually said, "It's like a battlefield down here."

At the time I thought he was being a little over-dramatic.

"Why do you call it a battlefield?" I asked.

"Come with me," he said. "I want to show you something."

Back in his office he showed me a surveillance tape of a losing slot player punching a machine. The player broke his hand taking out his frustrations on a helpless Double Diamond slot machine. On the same tape I watched a woman throw a hot cup of coffee at a video poker machine because she missed the Royal by one card. Most of the coffee splashed off the machine and onto her clothes. The only person who won on that deal was her dry cleaner.

The Battlefield

Row after row of neatly groomed slot machines dominate the casino floor. Their colorful, Windex-clean screens glow with pride and confidence. They stand shoulder-to-shoulder, tall and proud, like fearless soldiers waiting for the enemy to make the first move.

Some players are gentle and pull the handle slow and easy. Other use the hard and fast approach. Some players prefer to let their fingers dance across the machine's buttons like a pianist playing arpeggio after arpeggio.

Coin-by-coin, the battle between man and machine spins on and on, until someone walks away with a Purple Heart, or a pocket full of cash.

In every machine there's a jackpot waiting to explode. Like a time bomb, the jackpot clock ticks away the seconds, minutes, and hours, until some lucky player sparks the fuse and ignites the jackpot!

For the player, it's a glorious moment of sight and sound. Bursting with joy and celebration! The machine's lights flash across the casino floor like fireworks exploding their colorful magic against a dark summer sky. The ceremonial sound of jackpot bells echoes throughout the casino, like church bells cutting through the silence of a Sunday morning. Their inspirational tone rekindles our faith and restores our hope.

In a chapel build on odds, luck, winners, and losers, miracles rarely happen. But occasionally the gods of Chance do smile upon us.

And when the lights and all the hoopla fade away, the machine will reset the time-bomb clock, and quietly wait for the next player. But for the winner, the sight and sound of victory will never fade. Like a precious childhood memory, it brightens with age.

The minute we drop a coin into a slot machine's coin acceptor there's no turning back. We fired the first shot. We invaded the machine's turf. They've been programmed for victory, but they're not invincible. Sometimes they do suffer the humiliation of defeat.

Slot machines have the sophisticated weapons of modern technology on their side, but we can't let these mechanical gambling robots intimidate us. Let's not surrender our hearts and souls to these megabyte memory, technological coin-eaters. Let's put up a fight. If we go down, let's go down swinging. And if we lose, let's give the machine a few battle scars to remember us by.

Sure, we all know how to play the game, but only a few know how the game plays *us*.

FROM A LAS VEGAS DIRECTOR OF SLOT OPERATIONS: "We don't have the A-bomb, but we do have the E-prom. The E-prom is the computer chip that controls the machine's hold percentage. The players don't determine the hold percentage, we do. One of the ways we determine our hold percentage is by the denomination of the machine. (Currently, on the Las

Vegas Strip, the average hold percentage is as follows: 11 percent for nickels, 6.5 percent for quarters, 4.5 percent for dollars, and 3.5 percent for five dollars and above.)

"These percentages aren't written in stone. Some casinos might loosen or tighten their machines. But no casino is going to loosen a machine and get caught with its pants down.

"Listen, a player might win the battle, but we always win the war! And the reason we win the war is because players don't have a winning strategy. The common mistake that players make is not having their own pre-programmed hold percentage. If you're playing against an E-prom you have to think like an E-prom.

"To be a winner you don't have to hit a jackpot. You have to be strong and realistic. If you have the discipline to pocket a certain percentage of your winnings and walk out of here with a small profit, over the long term, you'd be a tough player for us to beat. Because basically, that's how we make our money. We work on a small win percentage because in the long term those small wins snowball into an avalanche. Remember, every bet you make in a casino is another snowflake for us."

FROM A CONNECTICUT SLOT SUPERVISOR: "The players outnumber us but we have the big guns: percentages, bankroll, and time. Keep in mind that every slot machine on the floor is a 24-hour weapon. So if the percentages or your lack of bankroll don't do you in, time will. We can afford to play against you around the clock. And if you don't know how to manage your money, sooner or later you'll run out of ammunition. And this is one war you can't win by shooting blanks at us."

FROM A SLOT DEPARTMENT MANAGER: "We try to keep players from leaving the casino floor by fencing them in with slot machines. Our floor layout makes it impossible for players to walk anywhere without passing a slot machine. It they want to eat, sleep, go to the bathroom, showroom, cashier's cage, or coin redemption booth, they have to pass a slot machine. We can't verbally tell you to play, but subconsciously we can encourage you to. By having an abundance of slot machines constantly staring you in the face, sooner or later the power of suggestion will whisper the word *Play*. We call it 'impulse gambling,' and very few players have the willpower to ignore the temptation."

FROM AN ATLANTIC CITY DIRECTOR OF SLOT OPERATIONS: "When we designed the physical layout of our casino floor, our main objective was to get the players in the mood to play the minute they walk in. We want the players to see, hear, and feel the excitement immediately. Table games don't have the visual or audio effects needed to titillate a player's imagination. That's one reason why we don't position table games close to the casino's main entrance. No game greets a player better than a slot machine."

FROM A NEVADA CASINO CEO: "You never want a player to walk into a casino and see a bank of empty slot machines. That's why we position our lower denomination machines in areas where there's a high volume of traffic. For example, every entrance leading into a casino is considered a high traffic area. When players walk in you want the casino to look busy. So we decided to put nickel machines in these areas because they attract a lot of play.

"We try to create a carefree, fun atmosphere. Because when players feel comfortable and relaxed, they play longer. And that's exactly what we want them to do."

FROM A CONNECTICUT VP OF SLOT OPERATIONS: "We try to make each area of the casino interesting and exciting for the player. By having a wide variety of machines, we have the freedom to position them in different areas, giving the players a mixed selection to choose from.

"Some players are under the misconception that we place the hot machines in specific areas. That's a fallacy. It's just one of many old wives' tales that have been passed down from player to player. Regardless of its location, every machine, in the long term, will live up to its hold percentage. Whether a machine is by the restrooms, main entrance, or elevators, the odds of hitting a jackpot don't change."

FROM AN ILLINOIS SLOT ATTENDANT: "Some players target the end machines because they believe we set them to pay back more. But that's simply not true.

It's nothing more than myth. Playing an end machine does have one advantage: MORE LEG ROOM."

FROM AN INDIANA SLOT HOST: "Location, location, location, that's the key word in the real estate business. But for slot players, the machine's location has no direct bearing on the outcome of their investment. For instance, in a particular bank of dollar slot machines, the hold percentage for each machine is virtually the same, so every player has a fair shot at winning."

FROM AN ATLANTIC CITY VP OF SLOT OPERATIONS: "Players put too much emphasis on the machine's location. They're looking for an edge, but they're looking in all the wrong places. The emphasis shouldn't be put on the machine's location. Instead, the player should look at the machine's overall potential.

"Before you drop a coin into a machine you should read and understand the machine's paytable. Because sometimes the investment doesn't justify the risk. Inspect each machine carefully before you jump into action. Look at a few different machines and see if there's a significant difference in the monetary value on the machine's low, middle, and high-end hits.

"Talk to the other players. Find out if the machine you want to play has a history of frequent low-end hits, but infrequent high-level hits. If it's a progressive machine, and the jackpot is linked to other casinos, does it play tighter than a non-progressive machine?

"If you're in the market to buy a house, spending time searching for the right location is understandable. But if you're in the market to find a winning slot machine, don't waste your time. Who knows, your dream machine might be the one with the out-of-focus screen, with the seat that doesn't swivel."

FROM A MICHIGAN CASINO CEO: "The casino floor looks like a slot machine smorgasbord. It's a coin-jingling, bell-ringing, feast-or-famine gambling festivity. The player's gambling appetite has changed. Table games are the little pieces of parsley that decorate the plate. And slot machines are the player's main entrees."

Bon appetite everyone!

Luck Is A Player's Ally

Players depend on luck and casinos depend on math. That's the cardinal rule of gambling. I'm sure Steve Wynn didn't spend $1.6 billion building the Bellagio because he felt lucky! Luck is iffy, it comes and goes without rhyme or reason. On the other hand, the mathematics behind every casino bet is steadfast.

Occasionally the dice, cards, or a roulette wheel, might go a little wacky and disobey the mathematical laws that govern them. Slot machines can also have a mathematical breakdown. Because when luck decides to shine on you, the heart and soul of mathematical probabilities become vulnerable.

FROM A COLORADO DIRECTOR OF SLOT OPERATIONS: "When you get right down to it, hitting a jackpot on a reel-to-reel machine has nothing to do with skill, but everything to do with luck. It's the old right-time right-place scenario. Machines go through hot and cold cycles. But they also go through lukewarm cycles. And if a player plays smart, a lukewarm cycle can be very profitable.

"Every pull is a random event. And previous results have absolutely no bearing on what will happen next. Slot machines are unpredictable. They fuel a player's passion for risk. Like the saying goes: "The bigger the risk, the greater the reward." If you want to be a successful slot player, disregard that statement. Don't be blinded by the larger-than-life jackpots. Never let a slot machine's jackpot bait you into playing. And if you hit a lukewarm cycle, cash out before the machine takes you to Alaska!"

FROM AN ILLINOIS SLOT SUPERVISOR: "Slot players actually believe that if they play long enough, their chances of hitting a jackpot will increase. That's a dangerous misconception on the players' part. The length of time you spend playing a machine does not necessarily increase your chances of hitting a jackpot. Long playing sessions don't increase your odds, they inflate ours. Whether you play five minutes or five hours, your odds of hitting a jackpot are the same on every pull."

FROM A CONNECTICUT SLOT ATTENDANT: "Some slot players are playing under what I call: the *due* mentality. Players truly believe that, over time, they're *due* to hit a jackpot. Or, if a machine has been cold for a few weeks, the machine is *due* to hit. Those are two dangerous misconceptions. Don't confuse luck with your inability to predict the unpredictable."

FROM AN ILLINOIS SLOT SUPERVISOR: "You can spin the reels of a slot machine 50,000 times and never hit a jackpot. But on the other hand, you can walk up to a machine and hit a six- or seven-figure jackpot on the first pull. That's the exciting thing about playing a slot machine. Everyone has a shot. Young, old, rich, or poor, once those reels go in motion we're all equals."

FROM A NEVADA SLOT HOST: "Losing streaks and winning streaks have no timetable. You can hit three jackpots one night, and play cold for the next five years. If you play on a frequent basis, losing streaks are unavoidable. It comes with the turf. But the key to being a successful player isn't knowing how to ride out a winning streak, it's knowing how to play your way out of a losing streak.

"Don't turn a losing streak into a personal vendetta. Anger is one emotion you want to avoid when gambling. Play sensibly, and above all, play a lower denomination machine. Don't look for that pie-in-the-sky, bailout jackpot. Take it slow and easy. Don't play aggressively when you should be playing conservatively. Pocket a few small wins just to remind yourself how good it feels to walk out a winner. Build up your self-esteem before a losing streak becomes your shadow."

I'd Rather Leave While I'm Ahead

FROM AN ANONYMOUS SLOT MANAGER: "There's something very hypnotic about a slot machine. Without saying a word it can draw you into a non-stop playing trance. You're not a bona fide winner until you walk out of here with your winnings in your pocket. If you win and you continue to play, you're setting yourself up to be a temporary winner."

Long, uninterrupted hours of slot play can, indeed, have a hypnotic effect on a player. The repetitive motion of spinning reels can captivate a player's eyes and rivet them to the machine's crystal-ball screen, until the unpredictable spin-by-spin process becomes soothing and tranquil. Eventually, the physical act of simply pressing a button or pulling a handle becomes a continual, power-of-suggestion pattern.

Hours come and go without fanfare or recognition. Coin by coin, the machines slowly take away the players' concept of time. It distorts the players' biological clocks until they become oblivious to everything and everyone around them.

When a slot machine casts its hypnotic spell over you, all your knowledge, skill, and common sense become blurred and ineffective.

How many hours you play, and how you pace yourself, can often determine whether you win or lose. We all know the importance of using a strict, money management approach to gambling. But very few players put a limit on their physical and mental capabilities. Physically and mentally, slot machines have no limitations. They have the endurance to break us down and the stamina to get back every cent they paid out.

FROM A MISSISSIPPI SLOT ATTENDANT: "It's really sad to see a winner go home a loser. But it happens. One night I was five minutes into my shift when a player hit a $4,000 jackpot. I paid the player and he moved to another dollar machine. Four hours later he was playing a 50-cent machine. Later that night I saw the same player at a quarter machine.

"He looked like a gambling zombie sleepwalking from one machine to another. There was no readable expression on his face. When I looked into his stone-cold eyes I thought I was staring at a mannequin. He just sat there pressing the max-coin play button over and over again. He was in a non-stop playing trance.

"Twenty minutes before my shift was over, I saw the player standing in line waiting to use the ATM machine. Obviously the guy was broke. The slot machines didn't beat the player. The player beat himself. What's the use in being a winner if you don't know how to act like one?"

FROM A COLORADO CASINO CEO: "If you want to increase your chances of winning, you have to correct your weaknesses before they become habitual. Repeating the same mistakes over and over again is inexcusable, and costly. Blackjack players commonly take the heat for playing incorrectly because their mistakes can have a negative effect on the other players. A slot player's mistakes usually go unnoticed because no one, other than the person playing, will suffer the consequences.

"With the exception of video poker, playing a standard reel-to-reel slot machine requires no skill. But it does require a high level of gambling savoir-faire. The biggest mistake most slot players make has nothing to do with the game itself, but everything to do with how the players utilize their bankroll.

"If your bankroll is small then you should play small. Don't try to jump-start a win by playing a high denomination machine. Stay within your range. And never play anything less than the maximum number of coins needed to win the machine's jackpot. If it's a five-coin maximum, play five coins. Playing only one or two coins might extend your playing time, but remember, we don't pay players by the hour, we pay them by the jackpot. If you want to conserve your bankroll, play a machine with a three coin maximum.

"Another common mistake is not following your instincts. If a machine is cold, leave. You must have the ability to walk away from a machine without second-guessing yourself. Never, and I mean NEVER, think that if you play a cold machine long enough it will eventually get hot."

FROM AN ILLINOIS DIRECTOR OF SLOT OPERATIONS: "Over the long-term, there are no sure-fire systems, playing strategies, or lucky streaks, that will enable a player to beat a slot machine with any consistency. There are no loopholes, loose links, or weaknesses in a slot machine. And players who think they've found one are making a deadly mistake. If you're looking for the weakest link, look at the machine's screen. And if you see a pair of bloodshot eyes staring back at you, you've found it."

Playing a slot machine is a headlong rush into the abyss of uncertainty. Casinos are a thrill-seeker's paradise, and every slot machine is a potential Shangri-La. But don't confuse your passion for risk with your desire to win.

Yesterdays

Last year casino profits from slot machines throughout the state of Nevada totaled over $2 billion. But it wasn't always that way.

Table games are beginning to show their age. Over the years there haven't been any significant changes in the rules, playing options, or table layouts. Traditional, green-felt-covered table games seem to be frozen in time. They haven't gone out to pasture, but the green grass of home isn't so green anymore.

Blackjack, craps, baccarat, and roulette were not conceived in America. They're European games that sailed across the ocean and landed on American soil. They were the pilgrims that started the gambling feast. But, it was American ingenuity that invented the dessert tray.

Born and raised in the USA, slot machines have matured far beyond anyone's expectations. They are no longer the casino's pacifier or baby-sitter for the non-table game player. Today, they're everybody's sandbox. And every player with a roll of coins has a chance to build a sand castle. Throughout America, millions of players are walking around with a little bit of sand in their shoes. And every neglected table game on the floor seems to be buried up to its neck in the sand dunes of slot machine mania. I have yet to see a casino executive reach for a shovel. Have you?

FROM A RETIRED PIT BOSS: "Gambling isn't about the cigar-smoking, high-rolling craps shooter anymore. Sad to say, but that era has come and gone. Presently, it's about the average John and Jane Doe, who sit in front of a slot machine for six hours, drink a few diet Cokes, and try to hit a jackpot."

FROM A NEVADA DIRECTOR OF SLOT OPERATIONS: "The tempo of gambling has changed. Everyone is in a hurry to make money. Especially, slot players. No other game answers a player's bet faster than a slot machine. The conclusion to every pull is instantaneous. And over time, the player's desire to see the end result of every pull will subsequently increase the slot player's game speed. Slot players who play long and fast are our favorite customers.

"Gambling isn't a race. Speed doesn't get you to the winners circle, endurance does. And if slot players don't have the patience and discipline to nurse their bankrolls, and pace themselves through the machine's cold cycles, they're never make it to the finish line."

FROM AN ATLANTIC CITY CASINO HOST: "I firmly believe that most slot players would be amazed at the amount of money they wager in one hour. For example, a fast-playing video poker player is more valuable to us than a $25-per-hand blackjack player. The speediest video pokers players will play 15 hands per minute. If they're playing a five-coin max, dollar machine, that means these players are giving us $75 worth of action per minute. Or, $4,500 per hour. On a lower scale, if we put the same players at a quarter machine, their dollar rate per minute is $18.75. Or, $1,125 per hour.

"The sheer speed of a video poker machine leaves a blackjack table in the dust. It's humanly impossible for any blackjack dealer to deal 15 hands in 60 seconds."

FROM A RETIRED CASINO MANAGER: "There's a generation gap on the casino floor and it's not between the players, it's between the games. Table games might have parented this business, but now their sons and daughters are taking it over."

FROM A MISSOURI CASINO CEO: "Table games use to be the blood and guts of a casino. I can remember when the heart, soul, and pulse of a casino used to center around our table pits. There was an interaction between the players and dealers. In a strange way there was a camaraderie between the players and casino personnel. We consoled losers and patted winners on the back. A slot machine can't do that, but obviously no one cares, especially the players.

"The players might have changed but the casino's main objective is still the same: Getting your money into our pocket. And no table game has pockets deeper than a slot machine."

FROM A MISSOURI VP OF SLOT OPERATIONS

"I think some players prefer playing a slot machine because it offers them everything exciting about gaming without the hassle of sitting at a crowded table. It's a one-on-one relationship between the player and machine.

It's one of the few games that respects a player's privacy. You can play fast or slow. No one's breathing down your back waiting for you to take a card or toss the dice.

"But, there's a price to pay for that luxury. I call it a `luxury tax.' Because compared to most table games, slot machines have a significantly higher, long-term hold percentage."

Slot machines have always been easy to play. Perhaps it's the simplicity that players find attractive. In its infancy a slot machine was a simple device: A mechanical arm attached to a steel box. Nothing fancy or glittery, in fact, they were boring. They were certainly nowhere near the state-of-the-art machines we see today. Slot machines are no longer the mechanical devices of the '50s.

Today, a slot machine is a sophisticated, computer-controlled moneymaker. With over 1,000 parts, the average cost to research and develop a new slot machine is around $1 million. Casinos make about 65 percent of their profits from slot machines.

In today's corporate-built palaces of fun and games, the term *one-arm bandit* is no longer in vogue. The corporate word is *product*. But I've yet to see a slot machine with the Good Housekeeping seal of approval.

And while the old one-arm bandits slowly rode off into the sunset, the dot-com generation rode into town with new and exciting ideas. With their technological know-how and Nintendo backgrounds, they reinvented the slot machine. Magically, they turned an old, dying, pocket-change game into a deeply devoted, born again, casino gold mine. Cities small and large are becoming slot machine boomtowns.

Like prospectors from the Old West, players roam from casino to casino hoping to strike it rich. Flight delays, traffic jams, and million-to-one odds can't dampen their gallant spirit for adventure. They labor away the hours in air-conditioned comfort, scrambling from machine to machine, hoping the next pull will bring them their pot of gold.

Today's "cowboys" and "cowgirls" don't carry picks and shovels, they carry plastic cards: Visa, MasterCard, ATM, and slot club cards. High-tech tools for a high-tech game.

Technology has changed the games people play. The power struggle over floor space between table games and slot machines is over. Dice and cards are no longer the Kings and Queens of this industry. Today, slot machines rule the kingdom. And slot players throughout America are merely their loyal subjects!

Are We Really Court Jesters?

Gambling isn't just a monetary battle, it's a mental one. Long-playing sessions can have an effect on your mental awareness. Bet after bet, like drink after drink, can be intoxicating. It can impair your judgment and give you a false sense of bravery. Sometimes the biggest joker isn't the one inside a video poker machine, it's the one outside.

Playing a slot machine is an emotional roller coaster ride of ups, downs, and unexpected twists and turns. Every pull is a breathless thrill ride that keeps us on the edge of our seat. Our hands clutch onto an invisible bar of hope until our knuckles turn white, and the spinning reels come to a screeching halt. But the real danger isn't the machine's turbulent ride. The real danger is the player's inability to know when to get off.

FROM A COLORADO DIRECTOR OF SLOT OP-ERATIONS: "Extended slot play can dull a player's senses and make them do things that they normally wouldn't do. One of the main reasons a slot machine can wear down a player is because the machine has no decisions to make. The game can only start or end when the player decides to either pull the handle or push the cash-out button. And fortunately for us, most players pull the handle."

FROM A NEVADA VP OF CASINO MARKETING: "When players enter a casino their first objective is winning. That's their game plan. Our objective is to get them away from their game plan by altering their senses. We control the gaming environment: air supply, light-ing, music volume, placement of table games and slot machines. We try to create a comfortable, carefree, re-laxed atmosphere. It's a subliminal attack on the player's psyche. Basically, once we get players on our property our goal is to keep them here as long as possible."

FROM A MISSOURI SLOT SUPERVISOR: "When players decide to play our machines it's the machine's job to keep them there as long as possible. There's nothing we can do to hold a player if he ran out of time or money. But we never want to see a player stop playing because he was bored.

"A successful machine has to stimulate players and keep them interested and hopeful. That's why machines that give players frequent low-end hits, or lower-level jackpots, get extended play. By keeping players within an inch of the big jackpot, we get more mileage out of their bankroll."

FROM AN ATLANTIC CITY SLOT ATTENDANT: "Even when they lose, most slot players walk away feeling satisfied if they got some bang for their buck. In other words, if a twenty-dollar bill bought them 60 minutes of play, they feel as if they got their money's worth. But if they lose $20 in ten minutes, they feel... excuse the pun, short-changed. Everyone puts a different price tag on their playing time."

Be honest with yourself. Are you there to win? Or are you there to see how long you can play. If you use your winnings to fuel your desire to play, sooner or later you will run out of gas.

FROM A DIRECTOR OF SLOT MARKETING: "We condition players to play longer by offering them comp incentives. The longer they play, the more we offer. Do you really think any casino would encourage players to play longer if extended play favored the players? Smart slot players don't give us unlimited exposure to their money.

"Never justify a loss by putting a dollar amount on your comps. This isn't the kind of business where one hand washes the other."

Smart players are like illusive gambling phantoms who hit and run, then silently disappear, before a casino host has a ghost of a chance to entice them into playing a few more hours, to qualify for the casino's "Gift of the Month."

Obviously, the main attraction of a slot machine is the jackpot. The jackpot is the star of the show and those little pay-outs are the machine's opening act.

Without a doubt the real superstars are the progressive machines with lottery-size jackpots. They give a low roller a shot at the big time. But they also take away a player's appreciation of a small win. Players don't want to nickel-and-dime a casino to death, they want it all and they want it fast. In a way it's ironic. Because most slot machines break a player down one coin at a time.

Indeed, a slot machine can be very seductive. No other game can wink at a player across a crowded room like a slot machine's seven-figure jackpot. It's like staring into the luminous eyes of a passing stranger, and wondering if a little harmless flirtation will end up becoming a fatal attraction? Or a million dollar love affair?

FROM A SLOT MANUFACTURER: "It's hard to predict if a new machine will be a success or failure. Some machines are an overnight success, and others never seem to get off the ground. When a new machine enters the marketplace it has to catch the player's attention. Something has to catch the player's eyes and ears. The slot machine's audio and visual effects can lure players into a trial-play session. That's the machine's bait. And if the players nibble on the bait long enough, hopefully the machine will eventually reel them in."

The name and theme can also attract mass appeal. Using the names of popular television sitcoms and game shows from the '50s and '60s, slot manufactures are zeroing in on the postwar generation. The newer slot themes are hitting the Baby Boomers right in their nostalgic hearts. But the real target is their wallets.

The pairing of television sitcoms and slot machines was a marriage made in heaven. Romantic? No. Profitable? For the casinos, yes. For the players... well let's not throw the shoes and rice just yet.

Companies that manufacture themed machines usually pay a royalty for use of the famous name. With that in mind I suspect that the payback on these popular theme-based machines might be a little tighter.

Player Vs. Machine

The interactive, multi-line, multi-reel video slot machines have certainly changed the relationship between player and machine. Today, players can have an interactive experience when playing a slot machine.

I remember watching someone play a machine called *Wheel Of Gold*. Facing the player was a back-lit three-dimensional spinning wheel on top of the paytable. If the "Wheelie" symbol landed on the third reel, the player hit a button to spin the wheel for a bonus of 75 to 200 coins.

Rather than just pulling a handle down over and over again, these sophisticated machines can stimulate players, and give them an adrenaline rush. Like video poker, these interactive machines offer the players a chance to take an active role in the game's outcome. **Interacting with a slot machine can make players feel like they have some control over the end results. And that's one of the machine's traps. The machine is giving you the impression that you're in control.**

CHAPTER 6

BlackJack,
The Big Lie

Blackjack is certainly the most popular and, at the same time, the most controversial of all table games.

History was made in Atlantic City when Ken Uston, a world-famous blackjack card-counter, filed a claim against Resorts (the first Atlantic City casino then known as Resorts International) after being barred from the tables. Casinos everywhere have since seen the immense popularity of the game grow year after year.

Slot machines are said to be the "bread and butter" of a casino. Blackjack, in its current state, is the main entree. And there's no sign of anyone going on a diet.

Where did this alluring game get its start? Although the claims are conflicting, three countries—Italy, France, and Spain—have taken credit for inventing the game.

Two games from France, *vingt-un*, and *trente et quarante,* give the French reason to believe they started the game. The Spanish say blackjack is an adaptation of a game called *one and thirty*. The game most similar to blackjack comes from Italy and is called *seven and a half*. From this game, the term *busting* was born. If players went over "seven and a half," they busted.

The game hit this country in the late 1800s. If history has taught us anything—and it always has—gambling, although illegal at that time, was never lacking for players. And players are always looking for a new game, new action!

To add excitement to the game, someone thought of paying players 3 to 2 if their first two cards total 21. If a player was dealt the ace of spades and the jack of spades or clubs, the payoff was 10 to 1. It is from this rule that the game was baptized "blackjack." Through the years, blackjack tables have been baptized with gin, scotch, beer, and other casino holy water.

Some people get very religious when playing at the seven-seat altar. "We call her the flying nun," says a dealer. "She plays black chips and usually buys in for $5,000. Before she signals for a hit, she tilts her head back and looking up she'll say, 'God, give me a 9.' Halfway through the shoe she was down about $3,000 and decided to leave the table. Before she left, her parting words were, 'God, I'm going over to the craps table because it's obvious that you're not in the mood to play blackjack today.' "

Casinos in Nevada legally started dealing blackjack in 1931. The game always made money... for the house! Players and even casino operators had no real knowledge of the game. Basic strategy for the player bordered on the ridiculous: rubbing a rabbit's foot on the table, playing a hunch, or a gut feeling. But the "ice age" of blackjack would soon melt in the Nevada desert.

In 1957, the *Journal of American Statistical Association* published a paper written by Baldwin, Maisel, McDermott, and Cantey. This report was the first scientific study ever done on blackjack. From the results of this study, Roger Baldwin wrote a book called *The Optimum Strategy In Blackjack*. Scientists and mathematicians applauded Baldwin's findings. Casino personnel joked, "Just another system to sweeten the pot." They had no idea that the joke would soon be on *them!*

If I were writing a book about American history, it would be impossible to omit Christopher Columbus. When writing about blackjack, it would be sacrilegious not to mention Dr. Edward Thorp, a mathematician, who, like Columbus, made a discovery. This discovery would change the rules of blackjack. Casinos would panic and rules would be changed. They all laughed at Columbus when he said the world is round. Over four hundred years later they would laugh at Thorp. Columbus laughed his way into history. Thorp would also laugh, all the way to the *bank!* Casinos don't like jokers!

A math professor from UCLA, Thorp wrote a book that would revolutionize the game of blackjack. Dr.

Edward Thorp's bestseller, *Beat The Dealer,* published in 1962, became a blackjack player's bible. And a casino owner's demon. Basic strategy, the ten commandments of blackjack, gave its apostles reason to believe. Judas would speak these words, *shuffle up.* A mathematician on a weekend trip to Vegas became the Walter Mitty of the gambling world.

Thorp, with the aid of computer expert Julian Braun, perfected a simple card-counting technique. He wrote a paper detailing every step of the process. Published in the Proceedings of the National Academy of Sciences, it was considered to be "the greatest achievement in game theory since the sixteenth century." Girolamo Cardano, the gambler-mathematician, won acclaim in the sixteenth century when he did a study on the laws of probability and chance.

In 1965, Thorp left one casino and entered another, Wall Street. His firm, Princeton/Newport Partners, trades so actively on the New York Stock Exchange that it accounts for more than one percent of its total volume.

Thorp's blackjack career ended when a casino drugged a cup of coffee he was drinking. "I got drugged twice and then they banned me from playing."

Like two ships passing in the night, Edward Thorp and Kenneth Senzo Usui (better known as Ken Uston), sailed the same seas. The course of their lives was about to become a trade-off. The calm before the storm was on the horizon. Uston, a former stockbroker and a senior vice president of the Pacific Stock Exchange, would chart a new course, a new life. Thorp, tired of turbulence, went searching for the calmer seas. One was bored by the casinos; the other was lured by the casinos.

The bait was the favorable playing conditions in Atlantic City. Resorts was not allowed to bar counters. Add to that: early surrender, four-deck shoes, and a ruling by the CCC that required Resorts to deal two-thirds of the shoe. Ah... 1979, the good old days.

Card-counting teams from across the country came to Resorts. "They're coming out of the woodwork," said one pit boss. "Termites, that's what they are. They're eating up the foundation. They're killing us!" Termites? A building is falling? Murder? A little dramatic, don't you think? Another pit boss joked, "It looks like a card-counters' convention in here. If I see water-filled balloons flying around, I'm going home."

Most of the "conventioneers" kept a low profile. But a few got carried away. Loud and boisterous, they were annoying the players, counters and non-counters. Gambling supervisors felt they were being ridiculed. "It's getting out of hand," said a supervisor, "They're jumping their bets from $25 to $1,000. A counter came to one of my tables about six hands into the shoe. 'What's the count?' he said. 'The running count or the true count?' asked his friend. They show no respect for me or my job."

Arriving in January, Ken Uston thought he would get a cold reception from the gambling supervisors. After years of being barred in Nevada, Ken was expecting the worst. In his book, *Million Dollar Blackjack,* Ken described the atmosphere at Resorts. "I wore a disguise the first day I went to Resorts. I'd never seen a casino so crowded in my life. People were waiting in line for a 10 a.m. opening. After playing a few hours, shift manager Rick Howe recognized me and said hello. 'It's an honor to meet you,' he said, as he handed me his business card. I thought I was dreaming."

The dream would end soon, but in the meantime, Ken and the other counters would be allowed to play unhassled. Resorts had 70 blackjack tables, and most supervisors feared there was a counter at every one. "It was like a three-ring circus," a former dealer said over a cup of coffee. "Counters were table-hopping, refusing to play against negative shoes. It was a floor show."

The floor supervisors weren't so amused. They felt the heat from upper management. The dealers felt the heat from the supervisors. A high-wire act without a net. But someone was about to fall.

"I was working day shift, and the same team would play in my pit every afternoon. One guy said, 'How long has this candy store been open?' *Candy store*, can you believe that?" Having a sweet tooth caused their downfall. The team went broke after three weeks of play.

Resorts knew there were counters among the thousands of players in the casino. Some were familiar faces from Nevada. Others went unrecognized. A physiological war was declared. The casino became the battleground. Resorts started the attack by restricting players betting $1,000 from playing more than one hand.

Phase two was lowering the table maximum from $1,000 to $300. Only a handful of tables allowed $1,000 limits. The counters felt the tension mounting. B-Day (barring day) was around the corner.

Phase three: Resorts started dealing six-deck games at the $25 tables. The counters attacked verbally, "These six-deck games are great. We could win ten times as much with a high count!" Uston called this a "smoke screen," because the fewer decks dealt, the better for the player. The smoke went out the window. Resorts wanted to see the "whites" of the counter's eyes. How do you trap a counter? Deal a two-deck game.

January 30, 1979: The war was over. Casino Control Commissioner Joseph Lordi gave the ruling that counters could be barred from playing blackjack. This brought a sigh of relief not only to Resorts but also to Caesars, which was due to open in six months.

Signs were posted on all blackjack tables stating:

"Professional card counters
are prohibited from play
at our blackjack tables."

If a counter disregarded the posted sign, a casino representative would read the following statement to him:

> "I represent the landlord of the premises. I
> am informing you that you are considered
> to be a professional card counter, and you
> are not allowed to gamble at any blackjack

table in this casino. If you attempt to gamble at a blackjack table, you will be considered to be a disorderly person and will be evicted from the casino. If you are evicted from the casino and return, I will have you arrested for trespassing. If you refrain from gambling at a blackjack table, you are welcome to participate in any other game offered by the casino."

Boston attorney Morris Goldings and Ken Uston challenged the Casino Control Commission ruling. They fought against the legality of Atlantic City casinos' preventing him from playing. Nine months after Uston filed his complaint, the CCC ruled that New Jersey casinos did have the right to bar counters, based on common law.

But the CCC finally came to its senses in 1982. It decided to make the rules tougher so that all players, skilled or non-skilled, counter or non-counter, would be allowed to play. Three rules were established:

(1) The cut-card could be moved to halfway from the back of the shoe.

(2) The house could shuffle the cards if the players tripled their previous bet at $25 tables and increased it five times at lower-limit tables.

(3) The house could shuffle if a player joined a $25 game with a bet of $200 or more in the middle of the shoe, or with $100 at the lower-limit games.

Uston eventually was hired by Resorts as a "spokes-man." Using disguises that once gave him access to the blackjack tables, he appeared in television commercials for Resorts. Surrender, anyone?

So, who are we to blame for all this confusion? The casinos, the counters, the CCC, the state? The finger points at no one and everyone. The casinos had very large investments to protect. Some counters "pigged out." The CCC was trying to protect the state's revenue that comes from the gambling tables. Who really won?

Presently, 800 blackjack tables a day deal eight-deck shoes. That's 6,400 decks of cards every day, or 44,800 decks a week. How about 2,253,800 decks a year! So, I guess the card manufacturers won.

Because of all the publicity surrounding the concept of card-counting, the game of blackjack has become the most popular. "Twenty years ago, seeing a woman at a blackjack table was unusual," said a pit boss at the Taj Mahal. "I believe that someday women players will outnumber men." He paused for a second and said, "I'll tell you something else. They're *damn* good players. Got nerves of steel."

I've become friendly with a man who's been in the gambling business over 30 years. He's a shift boss, and at his request I won't mention his name. Years ago, he dealt blackjack in New York and Ohio, in little "after hours" clubs. He went to Nevada in the '50s and worked as a dealer, floorman, and pit boss.

"John, what do you think would happen in we put 12 decks in a shoe?" A fair question. "The house would make more money and the tables would still be full. What if we dealt one- and two-deck games?"

"The house would still make money, and the tables would still be full."

"You're right, and I'll tell you why. The majority of the players don't know the first thing about this game. They have no respect for it."

Night after night, I've watched people approach a blackjack table as if they were buying a car or a refrigerator. First, they look at the price, the table minimum. Then they look at the salesmen, the dealer. Oh... he or she looks friendly, trustworthy, cute. Next they look at the customers, the players. Are they happy? If everything meets with their specifications, they buy in without looking at the product—the *shoe*. Are they buying a four-, six-, or eight-deck game? What they're buying is the *moment,* the *thrill!*

"Blackjack is like life," said one casino host. "Decisions, strategy, fate, but in the end we all bust. It's the in between that counts. Hopefully, the victories surpass the losses."

Some players might have to live to be 100, just to outlive their losses! "I beat a player one night for $180,000," said a ten-year veteran dealer. "He really beat himself. One of the worst players I've seen. A player like that should stay home and *phone* the money in!"

Blackjack never loses its sense of humor. This classic story comes from Vegas:

A lady in her late 60s was heir to a very large fortune. Dressed elegantly, she and her friends would play blackjack. Dealers welcomed her because she was very generous with her tokes. A good customer, the sweet old lady never caused a problem.

But her friends, they were another story. Her friends were four stuffed animals. And like her, they also played blackjack. She would seat two friends to her right and two to her left. She sat in the middle. After betting $100 for each friend, she would order drinks for her thirsty playing partners. "Give Mr. Monkey and Mr. Kangaroo a beer, Bloody Marys for Mr. Elephant and Mr. Camel," she would say without a hint of embarrassment. She would also sample each drink.

Imagine a waitress telling her husband, "Boy, I'm tired. I served a bunch of animals all night."

"I wish you could quit that job, Doris. Those damn casinos are turning into zoos."

Standing behind her at all times was her personal valet. After each friend was dealt a hand, she would signal for a hit. When one of her friends broke, she would give it a slap, sending it across the casino. Her valet would pick up the busted uh... player and return it to its seat.

One night she had a $500 bet up for Mr. Monkey. He busted, and she hit him so hard that his head fell off. Turning to her valet, she said, "Bring Mr. Monkey up to the room. He's had too much to drink tonight." Only in a casino, folks!

But how about the winning side? A dealer recalls a winning moment:

"The casino just opened. This guy buys in for $50. By the end of my shift he's up about $4,000. The next day he's waiting for my table to open. He could do no wrong and wins about $8,500. After three days of playing, he won $18,500. On a $50 buy-in, can you believe that?"

Blackjack, a game of technical skills, has captured the heart and spirit of gamblers by the millions. It is a game that proves itself mathematically correct when played properly and under the right conditions, but shows little tolerance for human error.

The plastic shoe demands respect from all those who seek its reward. The game continually puts our emotions to the test, from the five-dollar player who punches the table in frustration, to the $10,000 bettor who laughs at the game's superiority after losing a double-down.

Can The Game Be Beaten Today?

The paranoia over card-counters intensified in the '80s, making blackjack the most revered casino game in America. Even today, no other casino game has been analyzed, debated, or written about more than blackjack. Walk through any gambling section in your favorite bookstore and you'll see book after book written about blackjack. Creating the titles for these books seems no different than coming up with the titles for weight-loss books, and all the other vanity topics from sex appeal to body-building. Try these on for size: *Win $1,000 a Day Playing Blackjack*, or what about, *How I Won Millions Playing Blackjack*, or, using the buzzword of the '90s, *Getting Rich At The Blackjack Tables*. Whatever the titles, books offering you the "inside secrets" to winning at blackjack have dominated the field in gaming publications, even to this day.

The authors bombard the reader with charts, graphs, strategies, computer printouts, mathematical jargon, and, of course, stories and more stories about how they beat the casinos at their own game. Most of these books are well-researched. A select few can make you a better player. Knowing the basic strategy and at least something about card-carding can give you a slight advantage over the house, but only on rare occasion. The key words you just read are *slight*, and *rare*.

The main question to answer right now is, *Can the game today be beaten with consistency?*

FROM A DOWNTOWN LAS VEGAS PIT BOSS: "Right now there isn't a player in the world who can beat this game with any consistency. I wouldn't have said that 30 years ago when casinos dealt single-deck games down to the last card. And I might not have said that even 20 years ago when a good player could still find good playing conditions. We had no idea what card-counting could do in the earliest years; we had no countermeasures. You could say that at one time the game was vulnerable for the house. But today, we have at least four countermeasures that protect us:

"First, we can limit a player's bet spread. Second, we can shuffle up at any time we make the decision. Third, we can move the cut-card. Fourth, we can employ multiple decks."

Every countermeasure mentioned by this pit boss takes away a card-counter's advantage, or at least seriously challenges it. If counters can't make large bets when the count is to their advantage, if the dealer shuffles away a player-favorable count, or if the counter will see only half the cards or so because of a weak cut, the card-counter's advantage is virtually eliminated. And I don't even have to talk about multiple decks. The majority of casinos deal six- or eight-deck games. Although some counters actually like multiple decks because they claim they can enjoy an edge longer, the fact is, six- and eight-deck shoes tend to thin out the fluctuations that the counter is looking for. Can you appreciate that seeing a couple of aces fly out of the shoe has much more significance to a two-deck game than to an eight-deck shoe?

FROM AN ATLANTIC CITY CASINO MANAGER: "The press we received from barring card-counters was worth its weight in gold. The news that someone could actually win playing blackjack created a gold rush of wannabe counters to our tables. They read a book or two, practiced in their kitchens, and then came over here and gave us all their money! There have been a few great card-counters over the years, some in my place here, and yeah, some of them made a lot of money, but those days are over. We were naive back then. We're not today."

FROM A LONG-TIME COUNTER: "Scratching out a living playing blackjack isn't what it used to be. In fact, I don't think it's possible today no matter how good you are. The casinos are too wise. Independent trial games like craps, roulette, or baccarat are virtually unbeatable in the long term because the odds always favor the house. But at any given moment, the edge in blackjack can favor the player. The problem now is that (the moment is) too difficult to identify and too difficult to cash in.

"I get a kick out of these books that glamorize the life of professional card-counters. Believe me, there's no glamour. I know of no one who has gotten rich playing this game. As for myself, I made what you might call a meager living playing the game. Today, I think the best a player could hope for is to supplement regular income by playing a little blackjack. And even that's very, very iffy, to say the least."

FROM AN ATLANTIC CITY PIT BOSS: "Do you see that?" he asked me, pointing to the little plastic sign on the blackjack table that read: NO MID-SHOE ENTRY. That's one of the best countermeasures we have to stop players from jumping into the game when the count is positive."

What the pit boss was referring to is an old trick that card-counting teams have used over the years. A counter sits at the table, making modest bets until the count is very good. To avoid throwing suspicion on himself, he has a pre-arranged signal that tells his partner that the shoe is positive. The player's partner strolls over to the table and jumps into the game, making a big bet. The theory behind this is that the floorperson and pit boss watching the game won't suspect anything because the new player wasn't sitting there long enough to be counting down the shoe.

"We call them guerrillas," said the pit boss. "They jump into the game making a $500 or more bet while their partner is still betting the table minimum. If the guerrilla wins, he usually picks up his chips and leaves. Another guerrilla on the same team might be standing on the sidelines, waiting for the counter to signal him. It's not unusual for a team to have two or three guerrillas waiting for the signal. That's why we have the 'no mid-shoe entry' policy."

FROM A VETERAN DEALER: "There's no way casinos are going to let a system, no matter how sophisticated or mathematically correct, get the best of them. If someone came up with a system that could beat roulette, for example, do you think the casino bosses would just sit around and watch their money walk out the door? NO! The system goes out the door!

"We've already witnessed that with blackjack. There will always be some mathematician or computer whiz burning the midnight oil, staying up all night trying to figure out a way to beat a game. And when they do, the casino will turn out the light by simply changing a rule, or anything else, to counter the system."

FROM A LAS VEGAS CASINO EXECUTIVE: "Do you think for one minute that we would stock our gift shops with books about blackjack card-counting if we really thought that these books would hurt our bottom line? We've made rule changes that protect *us*, not the counter."

I was watching a $100-minimum blackjack game one night. The casino manager, who's a friend of mine, was standing in the pit observing the game. The player looked very familiar to me. I'd seen him at other casinos. He left the table down $800 in losses. Hours later, the casino manager and I met for our scheduled meeting. I told my friend that I recognized the player and asked him if he thought the player was a card-counter. That question started a two-hour discussion on the subject of blackjack. But the question that I feel got the best response was: **Has there been a scam going on between the casinos and the public with all the publicity on blackjack counters?**

He paused for a minute, added sugar to his coffee, and said, "We like these books and all the claims about being able to beat the game and about card-counting. Well, if I'm talking to the public or doing a newspaper interview, for example, I'll tell everyone that this game can be beaten, that we worry about it, that we watch for card-counters, and all that bull. Fact is, if I'm talking off the record, blackjack today isn't at all like it was years ago, because we've got good countermeasures in place now. We're not afraid of anyone. If you know some card-counters who bet big, tell me who they are and I'll send a limo for them right now."

He gave me the phone number of a retired dealer in Nevada who has dealt to everyone from Edward Thorp to Ken Uston. I asked him the following questions:

Can all this publicity about card-counters be a casino marketing scheme? Do card-counters really threaten a casino's bottom line? Is casino blackjack vulnerable? Can a player beat the game?

Here's what he had to say: "Until Thorp's book came along, players and casino personnel had no mathematical understanding of the game. All we knew was that blackjack, like all casino games, made money for the house. The basic strategy of the game as we know it today, did not exist back then. Players relied on hunches and gut feelings when it came to hitting or standing. There's nothing scientific about playing that way.

"Before all the rule changes, and the court's ruling that no longer gives a casino the right to ban a card-counter, a very few select counters did win. But for every counter who won, there had to be thousands of wannabe counters who lost. From my experience as a dealer, and I've dealt to them all, a successful... and I mean *consistently* successful... card-counter today is a myth. But for a myth to have longevity, a hero must come along once in a while. And, like Robin Hood and

Superman, casino heroes are becoming a thing of the past."

I would like to dedicate this chapter to Ken Uston, my mentor, who died on September 19, 1987.

CHAPTER 7

The Bigger They Bet, The Harder They Fall

Casinos are always looking for new high rollers. They send representatives abroad, mostly to the Far East, in the hope of reaping a new crop of "premium" players. But they also stay at home and look for that diamond in the rough right under their own roofs.

Casinos are often accused of trying to mold average players into high rollers. **They target the mid-level player, setting the most dangerous trap of all... an almost subliminal nurturing of mid-level players up to the ranks of High Roller.**

If you find yourself "moving up" the betting scale, this chapter will show you the dangers of playing into the casinos' hands. In his book, *How To Win,* venerable gaming author John Gollehon hit the nail on the head when he said, "Don't let the casino push you up the wagering ladder, especially if you don't like heights."

If you're a quarter slot player and you suddenly find yourself playing dollar machines just because you want to upgrade your comp status, you're taking a giant step in the wrong direction. Never let your guard down in a casino. Don't let the carefree atmosphere and comp incentives influence the amount of money you bet, or the way you play, or the length of time you play. If you want to climb the high-roller ladder, you're going to fall off.

Eventually.

Guaranteed.

The Myth Of High Rollers

Jerry Bock and Sheldon Harnick wrote the award-winning lyrics for the play, "Fiddler On The Roof." Set in czarist Russia during the eighteenth century, Tevye, a peasant farmer, dreams of becoming a rich man. "All day long I'd biddy biddy bum," sings Tevye as his fantasy of wealth turns rich in song.

There's a little bit of Tevye in all of us. Imagine flying to Paris for the weekend. Sailing around the world. Shopping on Rodeo Drive, where the word *sale* is a four-letter obscenity. Or how about heading out to Vegas where a $100,000 credit-line is just waiting for your pen. "Oh, the good life," sings Tony Bennett, "to be free and explore the unknown."

But what's it really like to be a high roller? Let me clear up the mystique.

Most people would tell you that high rollers are a constant threat to a casino. Most people believe that high rollers win thousands and thousands of dollars, more often than not. Most people often make the assumption that high rollers are the better players, even expert gamblers.

Most people are wrong. The win/loss ledger for these players looks strikingly similar to that of the average player, with that one exception of the decimal point.

For most of us, seeing someone lose an average player's entire net worth on a few hands of baccarat is mind-boggling. "I guess you can get immune to anything," said Linda, a floorperson. "When I first started in this business, seeing someone lose $1,000 a hand was unbelievable to me. Now, there are nights when $10,000 bets don't even catch my attention.

"We once had five baccarat players from Brazil betting $50,000 a hand. Halfway through the shoe one of our regular customers sat down to play. Two hands later he left. He said his $500 bets made him feel cheap!"

Over the next few pages, I want to tell you two stories about high rollers. The stories are more than just interesting. They show the casinos' traps at work most vividly. See if you can detect the traps while you enjoy the stories.

When you've finished, I'm sure you'll agree that the high-roller scene is one humongous trap that you don't want to get caught in.

Mrs. G

Everyday-wear for Mrs. G is something by Bob Mackie or Chanel. Away from the tables, the soft-spoken Mrs. G glows with charm and elegance. But at the tables, this five-foot-three-inch jewel of a lady goes right for the jugular vein. Like a tiger in pursuit of her prey, Mrs. G, sensing a hot shoe, attacks. Her weapon is the poison dart that all casino owners fear: parlay, parlay, parlay... when the dealer's breakin', breakin', breakin'.

"You have to know when to go in for the kill," Mrs. G told me, with a cold look in her eye. Tough talk for a lady who's over 70 years old and heir to a multi-million-dollar fortune.

"I only play blackjack and baccarat because I believe you can win if you're patient. Casinos are vulnerable to negative swings. It's up to the player to seize the moment. In life, patience is said to be a virtue. But at the tables, it's the calm before the storm. And I'm like a hurricane gathering strength with each winning bet!"

She's a poet and a philosopher one minute, and a gambler with a sense of humor the next. Emily Dickinson and Aristotle, with a *million-dollar* credit line! The sunken living room in her comped penthouse suite is breathtaking. A butler serves Mrs. G and me espresso coffee and Italian pastries. Mrs. G's personal secretary enters the room: "Excuse me, Mrs. G, Mr. G just called. He's leaving New York now and should be here by five o'clock."

"My husband isn't a casino player, but he loves the horses."

"Is he a good handicapper?" I asked.

"He doesn't bet on them, he buys them! Would you like to join us for dinner tonight? Nothing formal, just the three of us. Do you like Italian?"

At seven o'clock, with the sun casting dramatic shadows of the tall hotels, the view from Mrs. G's luxurious suite is captivating. Mr. G reminds me of George Burns, not in looks but in characteristics. "Did my wife tell you that we've been to every casino throughout the world?"

Mrs. G, wearing a beautiful and very elegant evening gown, enters the room. Her husband, with a sparkle in his eye, greets his wife. Hand in hand, they walk down the three steps leading into the living room. Love is forever young, regardless of what the calendar might say.

There are four gourmet restaurants in the hotel. but which one has Mrs. G chosen for tonight? The butler answered my question in three words: "Dinner is served!"

If you can't lead a high roller to the gourmet restaurant; bring the gourmet restaurant to the high roller. Two rooms down from the living room is a dining room. Complete with Lenox china, Baccarat crystal, and table linens from Italy. Two weeks ago I was drinking grape juice out of a paper cup in the employees' cafeteria 40 floors below the very spot where I'm sitting. But tonight, I have a butler pouring a cup of coffee for me and asking if everything is satisfactory. And my friends say I'm a starving writer!

"John," said Mrs. G after a delightful dinner, "let's go downstairs and have some fun." Mr. G decides to take a walk on the Boardwalk.

"I always loved walking the boards," said Mr. G. "A cool ocean breeze, the array of people. It's funny, but the older you get, the more you enjoy the simple things in life."

Mrs. G took one step into the high-roller pit and all hell broke loose. Suits with badges came out of the woodwork. Pit bosses, casino hosts, floorpersons, all converged around Mrs. G. The president of the United States doesn't receive this kind of welcome. But then again, the president isn't a $1,000-per-hand player.

Earlier that day, Mrs. G's secretary called the casino host requesting a $1,000-minimum blackjack table be reserved. The casino host, pit boss, and floorperson escorted us to the empty table. A dealer unfolds her arms and begins to shuffle. Mrs. G is sitting directly in front of the dealer.

Like any red-blooded American gambler, Mrs. G does have her superstitions. No one is allowed to sit next to her. If players want to join the game, they will have to be seated two seats away. Two chairs are removed from the table, giving Mrs. G plenty of elbow room. Reserved signs, like bookends, are positioned on her right and left side to ward off the evil spirits. Try this at a $10 table and the pit boss will probably break a mirror, open a large umbrella, and have a black cat run a few laps around the table. Being a high roller does have its privileges.

Mrs. G signs a marker for $50,000, orders a cup of tea, and lights a cigarette. She politely smiles at the dealer before inserting the yellow cut-card into the six-deck monster. "Good luck," said the dealer as she placed the cards in the shoe. "Thank you, dear," replied the table's only player. The cards are in place, a floorperson is standing at attention. Mrs. G is stacking orange chips ($1,000 each) into columns—$10,000 columns!

At the tables, Mrs. G has the stamina of a 21-year-old. A head-to-head game moves quickly. The hand is quicker than the eye; $40,000 in chips vanish into thin air. Shoe after shoe, hand after hand, marker after marker, cards appear and disappear like magic. Mrs. G plays flawless basic strategy, never losing her concentration. Her bets ranged from a low of $1,000, to a high of $10,000.

What two words, besides "early out," make a casino host smile?

"Marker, please." Without a quiver or sign of emotion, Mrs. G signs her fourth $50,000 marker.

"Fifty thousand," said the dealer. Her deep brown eyes are beginning to show signs of stress. The floorperson has been by her side keeping a constant vigil on her every move. A pit boss gave her a look of displeasure when she incorrectly totaled a six-card hand.

The eye in the sky never sleeps. Those 20-minute breaks do little to relieve the pressure.

"Fifty thousand," echoes the floorperson.

"Better luck, Mrs. G." The dealer's voice is soft and soothing. Her petite hands look even smaller as they gently move $50,000 in chips across the table. Except for her wedding ring, the dealer's hands are bare. Ten years of shuffling and reshuffling, and yet her hands remain soft, unscarred.

For those who stand behind the tables long enough, the scars run deep. Behind the eyes of every dealer there's a player, or a night, that just won't go away. The *real* players show compassion, understanding. Mrs. G knows that it's not the dealer who decides a player's fate, it's fate itself!

Fate costs Mrs. G another $30,000, but the player in her wasn't about to quit. At 4 a.m. and with $20,000 in her hands, Mrs. G sat down at the baccarat table. Once again it became obvious to me how important it is for a casino to have a player like Mrs. G. A losing player at the table was using obscene language. A floorperson walked over to the player, saying: "Sir, there's a lady present. Please watch your language."

"And what if I don't?" said the player.

"If you don't," said the floorperson, "I'll have security escort you out of the pit."

"What the hell is this joint, a church?!" No one was laughing at the player's sarcastic joke.

At $1,000 a hand, Mrs. G was the pope of the casino. At $25 a hand, the foul-mouthed player was flirting with excommunication! Mrs. G whispered to me, "He's a loser for letting his emotions get the best of him."

The third shoe gave Mrs. G the chance to "seize" the moment. Baccarat players look for streaks, or patterns. Choppy shoes are disastrous—a player's worst nightmare. Mrs. G played every hand like a sweet lullaby.

This was a "banker's" shoe, and Mrs. G was taking out a large withdrawal. Orange chips seemed to be falling out of the sky. There was no time to stack them into neat $10,000 columns. The shoe ended with a streak of nine bank-hand winners.

The cursing player, who at this point had nothing to lose, left the table with a flurry of four-letter words.

Pushing the chips toward the dealer, Mrs. G said, "I've had enough for one night." Mrs. G looked fresher than anyone else at the table. "This is for the dealers."

Five black chips went into the dealer's toke box. Earlier, at the blackjack table, Mrs. G also toked the dealer $500.

"One hundred and fifty-five thousand," said the dealer after counting Mrs. G's chips, twice. The crowd, which had gathered by the pit to watch the action, started to disperse. We overheard one of the spectators saying: "Look at all the money that old lady won!"

Mrs. G looked at me and smiled. She held my hand and pulled me closer. "John," her voice was soft, like she was about to let me in on a big secret. "I lost $45,000 tonight. To me, it's like going out on a date with the casino, dutch treat. Only I got stuck with the tip!"

Mr. L

Writing a chapter about high rollers would not be complete—in fact, it would be sacrilegious—not to mention the crème de lá crème of craps shooters from the Northeast. Metropolitanites, who were once the chiropractic backbone of Nevada casinos in the '50s and '60s, are now slowly fading away, disturbing nature's balance in the casino.

I'm talking about the two-fisted craps shooters who chew half-lit Cuban cigars. Guys who drink Johnnie Walker Black on the rocks and call every cocktail waitress "sweetheart." These guys are big tippers who throw $25 chips onto "Sweetheart's" tray, like a package plan vacationer throwing coins in a fountain. For luck, or for image? The "sweethearts" never ask. Years of long-distance walking across the casino has calloused their inquisitive nature. A thank-you toke and a smile can't heal their sore feet or aching backs, but it helps pay the bills!

We're talking action players who belly up to the green linen craps table, like a family about to sit down to a Thanksgiving Day dinner. The in-laws are easy to recognize; they're the "don't" bettors. As the dice pass from shooter to shooter, these pilgrims of casino gambling give thanks, until someone sevens-out!

Ever since the Camelot days of Vegas, craps shooters have hungered for two things: Sinatra and heavyweight fights.

"When Frank used to work the Sands in Vegas," said a retired pit boss, "the drop at our craps tables quadrupled. Our best players came from the Northeast. We also noticed a big increase in quarter slot play. We couldn't understand why the slots were so busy. One night a casino host figured it out. J. Edgar Hoover must have sent half of the bureau here to spy on Frank's fans."

On this cold winter night, the Boardwalk in front of Atlantic City's Convention Hall is bursting with energy and excitement. A large crowd slowly filters into the massive hall. Tonight is fight night, Tyson vs. Holmes. Ringside seats costing $500 are reserved for the casino heavyweights, action players with undisputed credit lines. High rollers, clutching their status—comped tickets—are rubbing elbows with Hollywood celebrities.

These craps shooters are from the Bronx, Yonkers, Long Island, Queens, Manhattan, Brooklyn, Staten Island, Philadelphia, Jersey City, Newark. Geographical neighbors, craps-shooting brothers.

Michael Buffer, the ring announcer, introduces the many celebrities and politicians in attendance. They get a lukewarm reception—polite applause, but not too enthusiastic. Only one name will bring this crowd to its feet. Everyone present will stand, out of honor and respect, for a man of courage and dignity. The announcer is pacing up and down the ring. He knows that the next announcement will create an avalanche of applause. A volcano of memories will erupt, from the $100 balcony seats down to the main level.

His professional voice suddenly becomes emotional. He's about to set off a verbal nuclear bomb. "Ladies and Gentlemen, the former three-time heavyweight champion of the world, Muhammad Ali, A... li!"

The applause drowns out the second "Ali." Heads turn, angling for position; everyone wants to see a part of history... a champion, a hero, a living legend. Everyone's eyes, glazed with emotions, focus on Ali. Cameras flash rapidly, like machine-gun fire on a darkened battlefield. Controlled bedlam ricochets off the iron and steel walls.

Climbing through the ropes, Ali enters what once was his domain, his fortress. His eyes hide behind a pair of dark sunglasses. Standing center ring, the aging Ali smiles. Hands that once ruled the ring seem fragile as he gently waves to his adoring fans. Tonight, the brutality of the sport yields to a compassionate moment. The toughest of men fight to hold back a tear. The bravest of men concede.

Fathers, who remember hearing about Joe Louis, or Marciano, will continue the tradition. Tomorrow morning, their sons will hear about Ali.

Mr. L, who promised to meet me after the fight, is sitting four seats away from "The Greatest." Mr. L is also sitting within a one-mile radius of $500,000—one-hundred-thousand-dollar credit lines, in five casinos.

The casino is quiet. Dealers, standing behind empty tables, stretch to relieve the tension in their backs. Cocktail waitresses exchange paperback novels. Bands play to empty seats. Bartenders read tomorrow's racing form. Pit bosses, filled with anticipation and nervous energy, sip stale coffee out of Styrofoam cups. Casino managers pray for an early knockout!

It took "Iron Mike" four rounds to answer every casino manager's prayer. Eyes closed, legs bent, Holmes hit the canvas. In a strange but melancholy way, this was a symbolic sign. One generation falling while another rises. Craps shooters, who once floated like a butterfly and stung like a bee, are hitting the canvas. Whether champion or challenger, no one escapes without a few bruises.

Telephones in the pits started to ring. "It's over, it's over," said one floorperson. Those two words seemed to echo throughout the casino. It took the casinos one second to knock out every five- and ten-dollar game in the house.

The heavyweights of casino gambling, the who's who of the high rollers, will be entering the ring any second now. They'll be knocking themselves out at $100-minimum tables; breakin' a sweat over hardways and double downs; stickin' and movin' in the baccarat pit; TKO'n' the casino host over comps. *If I only had money,* I thought to myself, *I could have been a contender!*

Mr. L and I talked on the phone twice, but never met face-to-face... until tonight. Sitting in our pre-arranged meeting spot, I heard a husky, rough-around-the-edges, New York voice, "Hey, kid, are you the writer?" The man asking the question had thick, black, curly hair, and wore a perfectly tailored suit. Nothing off the rack for this 74-year-old self-made millionaire.

"I gotta gang of stories for ya. See this hand?" Mr. L held up his right hand. "One night this hand held the dice for almost one hour. I made over $150,000, just on my roll."

A bragger? A showoff? Nah, just another $1,000 pass-line bettor relating another war story to an injured infantryman. Mr. L also revealed his battle scars. "I also lost over $200,000 while my wife and daughter sat front-row listening to Sinatra. I learned a very important lesson that night. You might wanna put that in your book."

"What's that, Mr. L, never stay at a cold table?"

"No," said a serious Mr. L. "Never miss a Sinatra show!"

Mr. L had a warm, friendly smile. And as he talked, I couldn't help but think that I've met him before. But where? Years of working night clubs called "The Silhouette," "The My Way Lounge," "Joey's Lounge," "Louie's Lounge." *That's it*, I thought to myself. I've met hundreds of Mr. L's, east side, west side, and all around the island of Manhattan. Guys who know that a winning night is only the eve of a losing night.

Turning to his friends, Mr. L said, "This kid is gonna write about me in his book. Say hello to my friends: Toothpick, Joey Doughnuts, and my brother-in-law, Tankie."

Joey Doughnuts told me, even though I didn't ask, that he was self-employed. Working those red-and-black color-schemed cocktail lounges taught me one very important lesson in human relations: When a guy named Joey Doughnuts tells you he's "self-employed," don't ask any more questions!

"It's time for me to take a shot." Those words flowed so evenly out of Mr. L's mouth. Like a guy telling his wife, "It's time to go to the office." Walking toward the craps tables, Mr. L stopped to watch a blackjack game. "You gotta be nuts to play this game," said Mr. L, lighting a cigar. "The table's loaded with kamikaze pilots. Suicide players. Guys hitting 15s and 16s, when the dealer's showing a bust card. These guys can destroy a whole table, and then go eat a lobster dinner without feeling guilty."

Kamikaze casino hosts began bombarding Mr. L with complimentary kindness. "Is your suite OK? Are you comfortable? Do you need anything? My best to Mrs. L. What can I do for you? Did you enjoy the fight?" BAROOM! BOOM! BANG! Mr. L is comp-shocked! And he hasn't made a bet yet.

Thousand-dollar pass-line bets, thousand-dollar come-bets, all with double odds, Mr. L had $12,000 laying on the table in 20 seconds. In 25 seconds Mr. L also *lost* $12,000. The dice went around the table from shooter to shooter. A pattern was being established: The point, a few numbers, and then seven-out, line away, pay the don'ts. Losing $32,000 at one table seemed to be Mr. L's signal to leave. "Let's go outside for some air," said Mr. L as he threw a black chip on the table saying, "For the boys!"

"Win or lose, I always toke the dealers, if they've done their job. Hey, it's simple etiquette. It shows you've got class! If I make a big score, I toke them real good. You gotta be a good sport, win or lose. Hey, there ain't nobody standing outside these joints pulling you by the arm to get you in here!"

The cold winter air on the Boardwalk seemed to wake up the philosophical side of Mr. L. "I love the uncertainty of gambling. I've shot craps in alleys, abandoned warehouses, army barracks, after-hour clubs, Cuba, Vegas. From cold concrete floors with some guy holdin' a flashlight on the action, to glamorous casinos. It don't make a bit of difference to me. It's the action, the instant reward.

"Whaddaya say before? I'm the last of a dying breed? You're right. Real gamblers couldn't care less if they're standing knee-high in horse shit or on some imported million-dollar carpet. When the dice are passin', any joint looks gorgeous. Those million-dollar chandeliers, the wall-to-wall carpeting, dealers wearing fancy outfits, it's a book cover, not the plot. If Atlantic City had gambling in the '40s—legal gambling—Vegas would still be a ghost town. Where else can you drop thirty-two-thou, buy a slice of pizza, and breathe in that fresh sea air?"

On to joint number two, I mean, casino number two. Casino personnel swarmed around Mr. L. "Good to see you, Mr. L. What can I get for you?" Mr. L, Mr. L, there seemed to be an echo in the room.

"The last time I was here I won $56,000. The way these guys are jumping all over me you'd think I won a million. They're Mr. L'n' me to death."

"Well, you're a high roller, Mr. L," I said. "They're just doing their job."

"See that guy over there? The one bitin' his nails." The man Mr. L was referring to was at the next table.

"I would never play at a table with him. He's a nervous wreck. He's gonna jinx the whole table. Look, he's got $25 on the pass-line, no odds, and he's sweatin'. Probably has a wife, a couple of kids, a mortgage, a car payment, mows the lawn every Saturday. That, my friend, is the foundation of all casinos. The guy can't win. He's playin' with scared money. Hey, put this in your book somewhere: Scared money is losin' money. Remember that. Casinos eat up guys like him for an appetizer. The least they could do is buy the guy a steak. But they won't. Do you know why?"

"Why?"

"'Cause guys like me get the whole cow!"

Here's how to get your own set of John Gollehon's personal Strategy Cards and save MONEY doing it!

The author's popular Strategy Cards have become the hottest cards on the market! The set retails for $12 in shops, but you can order the complete set by mail for only $9.95. Your cards go out within 48 hours and we pay the first-class postage!

BLACKJACK: Every player-hand and dealer up-card combination is listed, so you'll know exactly when to hit, stand, split, or double down. The Strategy Card does all the work!

CRAPS: All the payoffs for the bets you'll be making are listed so you can be sure you're getting all the winnings you deserve! A complete rundown for playing the game is also included.

VIDEO POKER: Follow a clever strategy to increase your chances of hitting a royal flush by 20 percent! The best paytables are listed, so you'll know exactly what machines to look for.

ROULETTE: A precise layout of the wheel is shown so that you can clock the dealer and predict the segment where the ball should land. See if you can beat the wheel with skill!

HOW TO ORDER:

Send check or money order for only $9.95 to: Gollehon Press, Inc., 6157 28th St. SE, Grand Rapids, MI 49546. Just write "Strategy Cards" on a piece of paper along with your name and address printed neatly.

Order your complete set today and start winning!